The Pismo Calamity

A strange tale of unnatural disaster

T. J. Rafferty

Chowderhead Press

2016

Published in the United States by Chowderhead Press.

Library of Congress Cataloging-in-Publication Data
Rafferty, T. J
The Pismo Calamity/T. J. Rafferty – Print-on-Demand Edition
ISBN 978-1520355146
1. Title

This is a work of fiction. Names, characters, places and incidents are either products of the author's imagination or are used fictitiously. Any resemblance to actual persons, events or locales is entirely possible, but will not support or warrant any non-fictional conclusion or fallacious syllogism.

Cover photographs by T. J. Rafferty
Book design by Brian P. Lawler

Manufactured in the United States of America
First Edition

for Bronwyn
as ever, forever

Also by T. J. Rafferty

Harley-Davidson, The Ultimate Machine
The Complete Harley-Davidson
The Indian
The Encyclopedia of American Motorcycles
Harley-Davidson, 100 Years
Ducati
The Achievers

Pismo Beach: a small town on the central coast of California.

Calamity: 1. extreme misfortune, 2. disaster. (misery, catastrophe, devastation, misadventure, crisis, ruination, desolation)

"When they went ashore the animals that took up a land life carried with them a part of the sea in their bodies, a heritage which they passed on to their children and which even today links each land animal with its origin in the ancient sea. Fish, amphibian, and reptile, warm-blooded bird and mammal – each of us carries in our veins a salty stream in which the elements sodium, potassium and calcium are combined in almost the same proportions as in sea water."

The Sea Around Us
– Rachel Carson

One

Dugan was about to quit the beach when he noticed the sport-fishing boat, moving slowly northwest some 300 yards offshore. Nothing unusual about the craft, but something… His attention shifted to a woman and dog down the shore when he took pause. What was it about the boat? He looked back. No more than three seconds had passed.

The boat was now slightly farther away, moving gradually into the sunset. Backwards. Dugan watched as the bow receded, at maybe 10 knots, and disappeared beyond the Avila Beach breakwater. He waited, mouth open, as if something else might happen, that an apparent anomaly in the space-time continuum might reverse itself, and the boat would cruise back into view. A circular hallucination, a phase shift in the linear transmission, like a freeze-frame on cable TV. Nearly a minute passed… Nothing.

The sun was slowly sinking down, and behind him the moon was slowly rising. The old world was still spinning round, and another song came to mind as Dugan pulled the Jameson flask from his pocket. A country tune on the jukebox at Harry's that very afternoon.

I tell you the high cost of livin'
Ain't nothin' like the cost of livin' high
Amen to that, brother, he said to himself. And took a drink.

By then the woman and dog had come within hailing distance. Dugan waved and the dog came running, an older golden retriever, as the owner arrived for the obligatory head and butt scratching, of the dog.

"Hello," Dugan said. "Did you happen to notice that fishing boat in the bay a few minutes ago?"

"No," she replied. "I was just playing fetch with Shirley, whom I see you've met."

"Let me guess," he said. "You named her after Shirley MacLaine."

"You're exactly right! It seemed she had lived many lives."

Dugan observed that Shirley appeared near the end of this one, without voicing the thought. But both dog and woman appeared to have plenty of energy. Salt air.

"We were out here yesterday," she said, "and she kept running back and forth along the waterline with her nose down. But I couldn't see anything she could be chasing."

"Maybe it was a cat from a past life," Dugan said. She smiled politely. The thought occurred to him that a dog might make a good companion these days. A pit bull, maybe. Call him Putin. Too obvious, on second thought. Perhaps a bull terrier, Satch, after his favorite character in the Bowery Boys. Or Satchel Paige, his favorite pitcher. ("Don't look back, something may be gaining on you.")

• • •

A self-made beach bum of some 20 years, Dugan had come to know the Pismo shoreline like a native, and read up on its history in his spare time, which was considerable. Between social security, occasional second mate duties on fishing charters and random gigs as what he called a "private assistant," he got by. And filled the empty hours at Harry's Night Club & Beach Bar or the county library. A competent but purely social drinker, Dugan had become a devout reader, able to hold his own at any level when it came to local history on the railroads, the oil business and the legendary Pismo Clam.

Business deals, legal and otherwise, not affirmed on the golf course were usually hatched at Harry's. The local hub for social and economic scuttlebutt, fishing stories, hookers and hangers on, the bar sat at the core of Pismo culture. Naturally the social mix had changed since the town's heyday as Clam Capital of the World. The bootleggers, east coast speculators and crackpot charlatans of the early 20th century were gone. The town, now landlocked by resort hotels, ocean-view estates, condos and the ocean itself, had shrunk as a get-rich opportunity for entrepreneurs. The Hollywood set had long since found other playgrounds, so Pismo Beach hung on to its early reputation as a good old sleazy California beach town. Dugan felt right at home.

Dugan James Byrnes was also sentient proof that alcohol still played a prominent role in the economic life of Clam City, as it had since Prohibition. "Thing about whiskey," he liked to say, "or alcohol in general, is that like most stimulants it's simply a matter of amounts. Someone said the only difference between a drug and a poison is the dosage. And the right dosage is something you can only learn with practice."

He wasn't a pugnacious drunk, nor one to bait or deceive people unnecessarily, to publicly flaunt any particular law, or to injure anyone who didn't deserve it. "Like, you know, somebody who hits a woman or a kid, that kind of thing…" But although his days as a club fighter in Pittsburgh were dim history, the instincts remained.

Back on his own stool at Harry's, Dugan contemplated the glistening caramel hues in the glass of Firestone Union Jack IPA before him. Meditation medication. The walk up from the beach had eliminated any doubt on the fact of what he'd seen, it just didn't fit the category of hallucination. But who would believe him, or even be interested? Occupied with these thoughts, he barely noticed the person who took the next stool. The jukebox was off, but somebody in the neighborhood had Ry Cooder cranked up loud

Feelin' good, feelin' good, all the money
in the world spent on feelin' good.

The crowd was light, mid-week, just this side of sundown. Hailing Henry, the world's best bartender, Dugan had reached a decision (Harbor Police or newspaper, maybe both), and thus earned another beer before dinner. At this the fellow next to him turned and said,

"Can I buy you one?" One of Dugan's favorite questions, like a lovely woman saying "Would you like to come in?" or "Did I tell you my husband won't be home till tomorrow?"

"Obliged to accept, young man." Not a familiar face. "You here for the Clam Festival?"

"No, but I heard that was coming up. Sounds like fun, but I'll be headed back down to La Jolla by then."

"Vacation?" Dugan asked.

"No, I'm doing some research on some… unusual marine activity here on the central coast. I work for Scripps Oceanography."

"I thought Scripps was working mostly on pollution and global warming."

"Well, apparently they had some sort of request from Washington, Department of Fish and Wildlife. They didn't offer many details." He seemed to be an earnest young man with purpose. The phrase marine activity took his mind back to Korea, many years gone. Not a place he wanted to go. "So, what kind of marine activity?"

"Well, I'm not at liberty to say, exactly. We've had some reports about uncommon events offshore, and they sent me up to take a look. Ever since that tsunami in Japan, some strange things have been showing up in the ocean." Henry delivered two pints. Dugan raised his glass to the young stranger. "Cheers, and thanks again," he said. "What sort of unusual events?" as he now considered a third possibility on reporting his sighting. This fellow might save him a trip to the police station or the newspaper.

"Well, like I said, I'm not supposed to comment, which is pretty unusual in itself. I'm just a biochemist, but I figure the government must be involved somehow. The Scripps folks are not usually so secretive."

"Interesting," Dugan said, already hatching a scheme to find out what the young man was up to. "Well here's an unusual event for you, that I just saw fifteen minutes ago. And it was really unusual." At which moment he glanced out the window as the last golden melting droplet of sunlight flamed out, escaping to the sky, followed mid-way to the horizon by a bright green flare of light, an emerald-shaped laser beam that came and went in a millisecond. Dugan nearly went stupefied again, and looked back to his new acquaintance saying, "What did you say we were drinking?"

"It's called Green Flash IPA," came the reply. "How do you like it?"

Two

Spence didn't know what to expect when he opened the door at Harry's. Just an old beach bar his diving friends had said, can get a little rough sometimes, but usually no weapons. No worries. After a quick scan of the bar for who might be the most interesting local character, he settled in next to a silver-haired senior who seemed to be transfixed by his beer.

The old guy was absorbed in thought, so Spence drank his own pint in silence, and when the fellow had drained his, offered to buy a round. They struck up a conversation which suddenly came up short when he asked how the fellow liked the beer. The old guy seemed dumbstruck by something outside.

"Ah…, it's real good, thanks. Name's Dugan, how'ya doin'?"

"I'm Spence. You were about to tell me about something you saw."

Recounting the boat story, Dugan realized he was now the one being interviewed. But it was what it was, and likely the best way to find out the story on his companion's secret research. If the backwards boat was part of some pattern of 'unusual events,' he was going to know about it. As his dad had said too often, "There you go again, thinking when you're not getting paid for it." But Mother Nature seemed to be giving him signs. "But I take it you're looking into stuff underwater, not on top."

"What makes you say that?"

"Your face. You've got goggle marks sunburned on your cheekbones, it's the raccoon look."

Spence laughed. "Yeah, I was in and out of the water a lot today. Went through a couple tanks. Buy you another beer?" shifting the subject.

"No thanks, only two before dinner unless I get an early start. I'm headed out, need a lift to your motel?"

7

"Thanks, no, I'm just up the road at the Sea Venture and I have my bike. Nice talking to you."

Dugan felt his old reconnaissance gene kick in, developed years ago in San Francisco's North Beach. His former job description, Personal Surveillance, carried a lower injury factor than Private Investigation, but was still hard on a marriage. He recommended Spence check out the farmers' market in San Luis that evening, as both a friendly gesture and a potential chance to creep the kid's room. Just part of his own research on curious marine activity. Gotta check every lead, stay informed on my own surf and turf. Material for the memoirs.

He left a five for Henry, and looked again out the window. The sky had faded to light gray against the slate of the ocean, a whitening fog bank inching along the horizon into the Oceano dunes. The Sea Venture. Appropriate.

· · ·

The desk clerk at the motel was impervious to his effort at charm. "I do have a Spencer Nolan registered, but he's not answering," she chirped. "You can leave a message, but I can't give you his room number."

"Ahh, jeeze…" Dugan whined. "We were supposed to go to the farmers' market in his car. Maybe he's in the bar."

"No, I was just coming on when he left. He told the other girl that he was going there. Maybe he thought you were supposed to meet him there."

Trying to appear humbly thankful, the part-time inspector ambled into the bar, where he was pleased to find they had buffet snacks. What Dugan called dinner. The knowledge of his new colleague's absence, and the reassurance of a beer, would be just the ticket. He asked if the barkeep had Green Flash. "Not at the moment. How about a Stone or Alesmith? They're both from San Diego. And help yourself to the buffet, this is the home of the perfect taco."

The recent proliferation of craft breweries was a fine and noble thing in Dugan's mind. Firestone Walker had become the big dog on the central coast, but in their wake had come a dozen serious brewers between Santa Barbara and Paso Robles. He was thankful to have lived long enough to partake of beer's new golden age, an achievement for someone who claimed being born under a Blatz sign. Surviving high school on Carling's, Pabst and Stroh's, he applauded the expanded craft in the brewing arts and dedicated himself to continuing studies in taste and character.

Then, just as he was at the end of the pint, and about to abandon the notion of a quick and mostly innocent search of Spence's room, she walked in. She wasn't tall or blonde, but she was something. Look of a cowgirl. Though he was the only one at the bar, Dugan flashed his best attempt at a Sean Connery smile and casually glanced at his watch, which he wasn't wearing. So he looked back, and gave her a wave that he hoped would be taken as invitation, and held the smile.

Which was returned. And damned if she didn't come over. Maybe 35 and cute as a button. Good skin.

He cut right to the chase. "Good evening, young lady. My name's Dugan. Do I look like you need a drink?"

She smiled. "I'll buy you one if you tell me where you got that jacket."

Oh boy. The garment in question, a brown goatskin flight jacket, an original Cooper A-2, bequeathed to him by his parents after the so-called Korean War. The one his brother wasn't wearing when his F-86 Sabre jet was shot down over Pusan in 1952. It was his favorite windbreaker against the Pacific chill at night. The geezer as fighter pilot.

"My dad had one just like that," she added. "I'm Jenny," she said and extended a nicely weathered but lovely hand.

Her dad? Dugan had all but forgotten the search mission to that point, when she asked what brought him there for happy hour. "Well, I was supposed to meet a young man named Spence," he fibbed glibly, "regarding his ventures at sea, but seems we got our signals crossed."

"No kidding? I met him right here at the bar this afternoon when I checked in. We set up an interview for tomorrow."

"You're a journalist?"

"Freelance. I'm on assignment for *Outside* magazine, doing background material for a story on..."

"Unusual events in the ocean?"

"He told you?"

"Only that that was his assignment for Scripps," he said, realizing he was about to be interviewed again, and took the lead by telling her the backwards boat story.

"That is very weird. You must spend a lot of time at the beach. Are you retired?" Dugan omitted from the brief bio his occasional role in confidential reconnaissance, but mentioned his local efforts in "classified research." That he had considered Personal Assistant as a working title, but decided it sounded too much like a health care worker or fitness trainer. And his only client on this case was himself. It wasn't curiosity that killed the cat, he liked to say, but complacency. That's why cats take that quick look over their shoulder all the time. They never know when the big dog's coming.

But Jenny Blake seemed sufficiently interested in the war stories, the rock 'n roll years, the peace movement, motorcycles and adventures at sea with tourists. "Well, you've had an interesting life," she said. "By the way, I'm supposed to meet Spence for breakfast tomorrow, maybe you should join us. And he's just down the hall from me in 302."

Hmm.

Dugan offered Jenny a solid maybe with high probability on breakfast, and said he had to be on his way so he wouldn't miss Colbert.

Then, after a stop to drain his beer, he checked the bar to see if she'd left, and headed casually to the third floor.

At 302 he knocked and waited a minute before pulling out his cell phone and punching up App UE-1.0. His last and longest military sidekick, Jimmy Burke, worked for one of those three-letter intelligence outfits in Virginia. Over drinks last winter he had confided in Dugan the existence of Unforced Entry 1.0, which opened electronic door locks without a card. The encryption program was top secret. While Jimmy said he wasn't permitted to share the app with non-agency personnel, he did leave his cell phone on the bar when he went to the head. Another leap for social media. And what are friends for?

Beep. The door opened quietly. The desk lamp was on, the radio tuned to NPR, and he recognized the soothing tones of Houston Person playing "Blue Velvet." In spite of himself, Dugan experienced a David Lynch moment, when the ordinary room abruptly seemed suffused in a dull, pulsating light, time expanding, suggesting the possibility that someone or something truly horrible could emerge from the bathroom.

But the moment passed, and the room presented only a large gear bag on one bed, a vintage long board on the other, a mountain bike against the wall and a wet suit hanging on the shower curtain rod. But on the desk was a laptop and a manila folder, so why not have a peek. With his pocketknife, Dugan lifted the folder cover to reveal a document with the cover title, *Preliminary Study on Possible Effects of Electromagnetic Radiation (EMR) on the DNA of Marine Life. (Code name: E/DNA. Classification: Secret)*

Below which: *Prepared by staff, U.S. Department of Interior, Fish and Wildlife Service, and California Department of Fish and Game.* And below that, penciled by hand in large block letters:

THIS COULD BE BIG!

Carefully lifting the computer screen, he saw a page from Wikipedia, with one passage highlighted:

> The effects of EMR upon biological systems (and also to many other chemical systems, under standard conditions), depends both upon the radiation's power and frequency. For lower frequencies of EMR up to those of visible light (i.e., radio, microwave, infrared), the damage done to cells and also to many ordinary materials under such conditions is determined mainly by heating effects, and thus by the radiation power. By contrast, for higher frequency radiations at ultraviolet frequencies and above (i.e., X-rays and gamma rays) the damage to chemical materials and living cells by EMR is far larger than that done by simple heating, due to the ability of single photons in such high frequency EMR to damage individual molecules chemically.

Hmm.

Three

Back in his modest beach house with breathtaking ocean views, Dugan opened a bottle of Deschutes Inversion IPA and a bag of pretzels. Settled in his leather recliner, he reflected on recent events and what he did and didn't know, and what to do next. Taking up his trusty analog Sony mini-cassette recorder, he dictated:

"July 22: The Scripps kid, Spencer Nolan, is not forthcoming, and probably doesn't know what he's looking for anyway. I figure he's just browsing in a specific area, looking for evidence of anything out of the ordinary, maybe monitoring a site where something was reported. But what...?

"Jenny Blake the journalist is friendly enough, but certainly won't be divulging anything that might get out before her deadline. Do wonder why *Outside* would send a woman ... might want to check her background. Neither of them seemed very interested in the backwards boat story, or were they just playing it cool? Or thinking what's this old drunk on about...?

"Questions: If there have been several unusual events in the harbor, and scientists and journalists are already showing up, why in the hell haven't I heard about them? No rumors at Harry's, nothing on the beach or in the newspaper... so obviously someone is keeping a lid on it. Time to check some sources. Maybe Mike Sweeny with the city police would know something, but couldn't say anything if they had an investigation underway. Worth a phone call.

"And finally, what in the wide world of water sports does electromagnetic radiation have to do with anything? What would be the source? And what sea creatures would be affected? And how? Tomorrow we go a-sleuthing."

Dugan disliked being out of the loop in his adopted home town, so the first item was finding who was keeping the lid on. For the name of the whom, he went as always to his native source at the Chumash Casino down the road. Jack Padilla, while not of the tribe, had sufficient native Mexican/American bones to sign on as a blackjack dealer. For some reason, Jack was always trusted with and generously offered all sorts of information from strangers. Maybe it was the customers' alcohol consumption, or the fact that Jack was flat-shovel ugly and people felt sorry for him. Or both.

But he was always charming with the gringos, and dealt a fair game. He was also regularly befriended by lovely young women, had a 31-foot Boston Whaler with a pair of Yamaha V8 outboards making 700 horsepower, and a full complement of diving equipment. Good guy to have in your corner.

• • •

The withdrawing boat story had Jack puzzled. "That is quite strange," he said. "I haven't heard of any boats missing so far, but if that was just yesterday… They could have been trolling in reverse for some reason, but at that speed…" But then he offered up a scenario more than its equal in weirdness.

"You've probably heard of Hector Romero, the diver?"

"You know I have, he's one of the best. Worked with Cousteau and Phillips, and then in features and documentary films."

"Same guy. Well he was here a couple weeks ago with a film crew, and they set up in Oceano and had a camera-rigged dive boat offshore. Three-man crew, couple cameramen and the director. And Romero.

"So, you've seen his picture right, that chiseled Aztec profile and long black hair, and he's gotta be about 60. Anyway, as I heard it from one of the crew, something bumped the boat, not hard but noticeable, maybe a whale. And a few seconds later, this guy says, Romero came out of the water screaming, terrorized, and completely incomprehensible. But it was his other aspect that showed he'd had quite a fright."

"What, I suppose his hair had turned white?"

"No, his hair was still black. This guy said his skin was white. Told me the dude went in the water a Coppertone red man and came out a white man. Hard to believe."

As Dugan pondered that unusual event, Jack added another, that he said was just rumor rather than a first-hand report. Story was that two buggies were rat-racing in the dunes, two guys in each one. The first one went airborne over a crest, and the other guys thought they could go around and reach the other side right on 'em. When they got there, no more than a few seconds they said, the two guys were sprawled in the sand and the buggy was gone. Disappeared. Said something hit them in mid-air and pitched 'em out, idiots weren't even wearing seat belts."

Dugan and Jack agreed that come Monday, his day off, they'd take the boat out for a look around. No women, maybe a few beers, just the two of them on a recreational ride. With instruments and recording equipment.

The plan gave Dugan a few days to check with his contacts in the agencies that had to be involved; the cops, harbor police and Coast Guard. And time to savor his renewed engagement in the active life of the town. Given the recent lunacy in the federal government, it felt good the get your teeth into something you could get your teeth into. A person can't live on bullshit alone, he concluded, which seemed to be the biggest chunk of the country's current information diet.

A sense of near-reverie ensued. How could it be, Dugan pondered, that he'd come to such a pleasant stage of life this late in the game. Probably just luck, he figured. His own favorite example of which was winning the street cred sweepstakes at Harry's not long after he first came to town. An annoying college kid, some sort of jock, was trying to entertain a couple girls at the pool table. Wasn't that he was too loud, just full of himself, but when he shouldered up to the bar and spilled Dugan's beer, that was enough.

"You owe me a beer, buckaroo," he said.

"Fuck off, old man," he replied, which earned him a shove and gave Dugan room to stand up. Then, almost as if the scene went into slow motion, the kid struck the kung fu pose and went into the spin/ head-kick routine. Dugan simply ducked, and just as the shoe cleared his head brought a left hook from the floor squarely into the lad's nuts. The punch, aided by the kick's momentum, spun him horizontal and ass first onto the pool table. He appeared to be in considerable pain, but unable to make a sound. Shortly he emitted a few soft barks, rather like a harbor seal pup.

The injured party rolled to his side, gasping, locked in the fetal position. Whereupon Dugan removed the kid's wallet and took out a five, then using the wallet as a mitten, stuck it into the guy's open mouth and dragged him off the table and out the door. On the sidewalk he replaced the wallet, leaned over and said, "You need to find another place to drink. Next time I'll take you out by the nostrils."

Back at the bar the adrenaline drained away gradually, replaced by an odd sense of surprise at his violent reaction. What the hell was that? But Dugan's extended good fortune became the blessing of never again having to live up to his reputation, so he counted it lucky to have that in place before he was too old for such crap. When asked about it recently by a newcomer, who might just buy him a beer for the story, he just said, "Well, you know, sometimes things just make you real angry."

Now and then he did notice someone nodding toward him, and once overheard a stage whisper, "Whatever you do, don't spill his beer." Everyone within earshot laughed. It was good to feared, long as you didn't take advantage.

Four

Spence returned early from the farmers' market since tomorrow was another work day, but first checked the bar to see if Jenny was there. Just a few business suits, happy hour refugees and one guy who looked like a surfer. Who maybe knew something.

"Get any good rides today?" he asked, settling in at the bar.

"Not many, it was pretty dirty and inconsistent. But my only chance to get out this week. Yourself?"

"No, I've been working all day. You surf here on a regular basis?"

"Yeah, I actually work here, renting boogie boards and stuff. I'm just waiting for my girlfriend to get off work."

"Let me ask you, I'm doing some research for work, have you seen anything really unusual out on the water lately? Anything that didn't fit the regular pattern?"

"Funny you should ask. The other day I was out before work, just laying on my board, and had my iPod and headphones, you know, it was dead calm... so I'm layin' there, listening to J.J. Cale, right? Tide's just coming in, and I start to move to the south, slowly. So I look around and it's still stone flat to the horizon, ain't a wave around 'cept the one I'm on. And it starts gaining speed.

"So, I'm out only maybe 70-80 yards, right, and this swell begins gathering some real velocity and I'm up. Now I'm way over by the point, like the north edge of Shell Beach, and within a few seconds I'm haulin' ass, man, riding the lip of the curl at like twelve feet, and it doesn't show any sign of dumping out. Flat bookin'! But here's the real weird thing, this wave wasn't coming in at the normal angle, which is like 300 degrees from the northwest usually. It was running oblique, almost parallel to the beach, and I came ashore, still up on the board in six inches of water, right at the base of the pier. That's about half a mile, and I was up and down the face of that puppy about thirty times, maybe 50 miles an hour max. It was like a freak solo groundswell. At the end it seemed like a dream, dude. Out'a nowhere, the perfect wave."

If that didn't have Spence sufficiently mystified, and more envious of a surfing experience than he could recall, into the bar walked the most beautiful black girl, or girl of any color anywhere any time, he'd ever seen. And she came directly over, gave the surfer a quick peck on the lips, and said to Spence, "Hi, I'm Pearl. What sort of tall tale is Hank telling you?"

As Spence struggled to regain the power of speech, his new best friend Hank said he'd just recounted his long ride across the bay.

"Maybe you can join us sometime," he said. "Pearl and I know a few good spots that don't get too crowded, one up near Cayucos and a couple just south of here."

"What about Avila Beach?" he asked.

"Rarely any good up there, too well protected. On the north side of Point San Luis there used to be some good surf, but they put in a breakwater for the nuclear power plant and that went away. Not allowed out there anyway. Morro Bay still gets some good sets though."

"Cool deal," said Spence. "Maybe next time I'm here. You guys headed out for dinner?" hoping that maybe Hank had a part-time job elsewhere.

"No," Pearl said, "we have to meet a reporter over at the Cool Cat Cafe by the pier. She came to see me in the office at school, about an interview, a story for some magazine."

"Would her name be Jenny?"

"Why yes, do you know her?"

"Met her here yesterday. We're supposed to meet for breakfast tomorrow. We may be part of the same story. Tell her Spence said hello. By the way, do you work at Cal Poly?"

"Sort of," she said. "I'm a graduate assistant in Marine Biology, and working on a degree there. Slowly. And yourself?"

"I work as a biochemist for the Scripps Institution of Oceanography. The job involves a lot of marine research as a diver, free and self-contained varieties, no deep water stuff so far."

"Well I'll be dogged," she said, "we have our own pier now at Avila, by we I mean the university, with a lab. We may have some things to talk about, besides surfing. Here's my card if you want to get in touch."

Spence so wanted to get in touch that he could scarcely say, but did say thanks I will as Pearl and Hank took their leave. He could not recall ever having a research trip that produced such lovely results, preliminary as they might be. He wondered if Dugan had any connections with the hotel chain's management, maybe see if he could get Hank transferred to the Honolulu branch.

• • •

Jenny Blake took a corner booth at the cafe and opened her laptop. The horizon displayed no spectacular sunset as the sky, ocean and beach slowly dissolved into a light gray monochrome backdrop to the town. The magazine assignment had been a bit of surprise, and the short deadline. Not a byline story of her own, but a good reference in any case. Paying work. Living nearby in Paso Robles helped, and she had a reputation for working quickly. She was also good with horses, and adventurous people. The magazine would send a photographer if she came up with anything tangible.

In less than a week she had covered local history on the run. She already knew that the railroad, at the tail end of the 19th century, had brought the flush of newcomers, largely from Switzerland, Portugal, Ireland and Italy, who joined the Spanish in colonizing the coast. Most of the Chumash tribes became farm and construction laborers, or working wards of the Catholic missions.

The political history barely figured in, beyond enabling oil companies to occupy much of the finest landscape on the coast. Between the drillers, the energy consumption/disposal traits of the railroad, the chromium mines, and the runoff from crop and livestock farms, the collective detritus all ran downhill to the ocean. Now, the industries of the century past had been all but completely eclipsed by wine grapes, as vineyards covered the valleys and nearly reached the shore. After four years of drought the water table had plunged. Desalination projects were back on the table.

But for Jenny the point of historical interest was the Pismo clam. The cute crustacean had been a seafood staple for the Chumash and their successors, and the harvest was bountiful. Families arrived in wagons and trucks from Bakersfield and Santa Barbara, commercial diggers dragged the beach with plows. On one day in 1948 the beach at Pismo hosted 150,000 clammers, who collectively found, dug up and hauled away some 75,000 pounds of clams. Perhaps the biggest and most delicious beach party in history.

But by the 1980s, between humans and the protected and prolific sea otter population, the clam was all but gone, followed, albeit at a slower rate, by the abalone. The Pismo Clam (*Tivela stultorum*) was kin to the family called Venus Clams, and was easily scooped from the sand. The abalone, by contrast, was a more muscular mollusk that clung tightly to rock faces, and required a diver with a prying tool. The first abalone divers developed better underwater safety and breathing gear in these waters, and many went on to jobs as military "frogmen." In the ensuing generation the frogmen became seals. Evolution.

Jenny was organizing her notes, separating items by subject, labeling new folders, when Pearl arrived in the company of a young man with astonishingly yellow hair.

Five

The window above Dugan's kitchen sink framed a view from Point Conception in the south to Point San Luis, the tip of the mountainous headland arc sheltering Avila Beach. Just beyond the north face of the reach lay the Diablo Canyon nuclear power plant, and just offshore the Hosgri Fault, an 85-mile lateral strand of the San Andreas, 2.5 miles out running parallel to the coastline. A little sister cleft, the Shoreline Fault, sat a mile from the plant. At the rim of a small cove a few miles north was a commercial abalone farm.

The public radio news reported that oil companies were drilling fracking wells in the Santa Barbara channel. The next story cited evidence that radioactive particles, generated by the Fukushima nuclear plant disaster in Japan, had been identified in rain water on the California coast. Dugan switched the station to KPIG, playing one of his favorites, "Gone Away" by Steve Ripley:

Cassius Clay/Muhammad Ali, float like a butterfly-sting like a bee,
JFK and Marilyn Monroe, John and Paul and George and Ringo
Collectively... Gone away,
Tumbleweeds blow through my hometown
And all my friends for miles around...
Gone away, All gone away...

Jack had said the Chumash called Point Conception the Western Gate, where departing souls passed between earth and heaven. Thirty-five years ago they joined other tribes to occupy the site to protest its development for liquefied natural gas production. Though he was a skeptic on various tribal myths and customs, Jack admired the Chumash. "They were a peaceful bunch, man," he said. "They didn't spend a lot of time fighting other tribes, they just hunted and fished, took care of their families.

"Maybe it was mostly the environment, like having the best

weather on the coast, and the terrain. You know, kind'a hard to stay pissed off in a beautiful place."

Dugan appreciated Jack's perspective, and didn't bother noting that the era he described pre-dated the arrival of the gringos, when things began to change quickly. But you get what you're given, and see about the rest. Still a fine place to be on the planet, he observed, though something was obviously going awry, and it was time to bump-start the inquiry.

...

His mind kept returning to the fishing boat. Only two ways it could have done that he figured; one was on an outbound swell more powerful than it's engine (assuming it was operable), or it was being towed out to sea. By something beneath the surface. In a personal moment in need of some levity, Dugan had to wonder if someone on board may have turned to the captain and said they were going to need a bigger boat.

As was his habit, Dugan decided one beer at Harry's would settle the thought process, followed by a walk on the beach at sunset with his imaginary dog Satch. Thence home to grill some salmon, have a glass of Edna Valley pinot, tape some more notes. Mayhaps swing by the marina on the way, see if anyone had heard of a boat gone missing. Virgil Crocker, the former city fire chief, had lived aboard his ketch down there for years, and would likely be the first call.

Dugan saluted Henry with a glass of Coronado Idiot IPA and set to pondering. Would be nice to have a bug under the table at the Cool Cat, eavesdrop on the three youngsters. But it seemed they were only a bit less shy of facts than he was, and a bug would be uncomfortably close to government work. Best to collect the necessary information the old fashioned way, straightforward questions, face to face, with some flexibility for minor subterfuge. And there was always Google.

Two guys at the end of the bar were engaged in an animated but polite debate on the subject of genetically modified foods. Dugan could have helped overhearing, but chose not to. As an interested citizen, maybe learn something... At a pause in the dialogue he leaned in. "Excuse me fellas, couldn't help overhearing... I think I know what genetic engineering is, but wonder if you could give me the basic definition."

"Well basically it's the biological alteration of an organism's genome, its DNA," said one. "In agriculture the object is to create disease-resistant crops that can be produced consistently, and economically. We've been eating genetically modified foods for twenty years."

"I'm hip to that," Dugan said. "What about the human side of the picture?"

"Do you mean as in cloning?" asked the other.

"No, I mean the accidental modification of genes by external forces, like unidentified toxins, or contaminated water, or radiation, whatever."

"So you don't mean genetic engineering, you mean what about the possibility of random mutations."

"Well, aren't we all?" Dugan replied.

"Aren't we all what? Concerned?"

"Random mutations. We're all genetically modified organisms, right? Our parents' genes combined to make us a new double helix. So we are modifications of modifications, and we develop new traits every generation. Evolution as they call it. We each get a new genetic code, a new language that runs our operating system. But what worries me is how that genome – yours, mine or that of any other animal–can be modified by the chemical byproducts of the environment it has constructed."

The men regarded Dugan with a curious gaze, as if he had either uttered something unexpectedly wise, or that he was a delusional old fart and a possible danger to himself and the public at large. Hard to tell.

"Anyway," he said, now on a roll. "Getting back to clones. Would they still be called drones if they were flown by clones?" Their brows furrowed.

Dugan bid the debaters farewell and headed for the marina. Sure enough, Virgil was on deck, in the company of a nicely dressed couple, and waved him aboard. Introductions were made, Mr. and Mrs. Reynolds, Santa Barbara… nice to meet you, sorry to interrupt… He begged off on the offer of a drink, just on his way home, etc., and wondered if Virg had heard of any MIAs.

"Funny you should ask. The Coast Guard cutter towed some guys in this morning, in a Hatteras 36. They had food and water, but no fuel or radio. I guess a charter pilot saw their flare and called it in; they were about 250 miles out, drifting southwest."

"How long?"

"Three days. They didn't say much to anybody at the dock, Coast Guard hustled 'em off in a van. And there was another car, with guys wearing suits. Shoulder holsters and short hair. Weird."

"Do you know who the fishermen were?"

"Do not, but they weren't local. The boat was from Marina Del Ray, looked like a first-class rig. There was one curious thing, though. I ran into Jake LeBlanc at the Splash Cafe at lunch, told him about it, and he remembered seeing them go out on Tuesday, and said he saw three guys aboard."

"How many got off?"

"Two."

Six

Jenny had no problem getting acquainted with Pearl and Hank, given their common bonds as locals, surfers and unreconstructed water babies who couldn't stay away from the coastline.

"The ocean is an abiding reassurance," Hank proclaimed, "even though we know we can't go back permanently, we have to stay connected." Jenny wrote it down. Everyone was on board with species protection across the spectrum, despite Hank's reference to sea otters as ocean rats, and the real reason for the near-extinction of the clams. Concerns were likewise mutual on the suspicious mechanics of the Coastal Commission and its political mix. The environmental framework was clearly being modified by commercial interests.

"So you're in the north county?" Pearl asked.

"Not far north, out near Pozo, south of the Sea of Grapes. And you guys?"

"We live in Oceano, we're Dunites." Jenny laughed. "Is that sort of like hobbits?"

Hank and Pearl chuckled. "In a way it is," she said. "We don't actually live in the dunes like the group back in the twenties. It was sort of a pre-hippie commune, and they lived mostly on clams and vegetables from the Japanese farms in Nipomo."

"Some of which they stole," said Hank, "but most of which they traded for clams. And by then there were fines for poaching on the beach. The Dunites had some clever ploys."

"I've read bits of the story," Jenny said. "Weren't they strict vegetarians, and vowed to not eat anything with a face?"

"True," said Pearl. "That came from their connection with the Ascended Masters of Mount Shasta, who were descendants of the Lumerians, who were part of the great Mukalian Empire." Jenny thought oh my, I'm stuck with a couple new age wackos.

"She's not making this stuff up." Hank said. "Some of the Dunites were just wandering beach creatures and squatters, but others were serious seekers, artists and writers. They could see where things were headed after the war, and decided to opt out and live off the grid. They had fresh water, clams, fish and vegetables. Life was good."

"They called themselves a community of individuals," said Pearl. "But what united them more than anything was opposition to war. They rejected the notion of world war before it had a number attached to it, so they were probably the first organized secular American pacifists of the 20th century. Well, semi-organized. And a few were deserters, from Germany and America."

"That must have been an interesting social experiment," offered Jenny.

"They had quite mix of folks," said Hank. "The primary dude was a guy named Gavin Arthur, who had money, and a grandpa who'd been president of the USA, Chester Alan Arthur. But the spiritual force was a woman from Ireland, Ella Young, who named the community Moy Mell, which is Gaelic for Pastures of Honey."

"That woman was proof that goddesses still roamed the earth," Pearl said. "She shared with native Americans that sensitivity to power places, specific locations where spirits of the past gather. In Ireland she was part of the literary crowd, William Butler Yeats and Maud Gonne. Many of the best American artists of the time visited the Dunites, people like Ansel Adams, Robinson Jeffers and Edward Weston."

"Later a more organized spiritual group, the Theosophists, built a temple over in Halcyon," Hank said. "So they were acquainted with John Varian as well, but as a group the Dunites were gone by the Forties. A few devout souls did still live there into the Seventies."

"Wasn't John the father of the Varian brothers, who developed new radar technology in the Thirties?" Jenny asked. "He was," said

Pearl. "That was Russell and Sigurd, and their work led directly to new medical equipment, CAT scans and stuff."

"So, do you guys hope to revive the Dunite community?"

"No, those days are history," said Pearl, "at least where the dunes are concerned. The state created the RV park designation a long time ago, and the majority public sentiment favors having a beach to drive on."

"It's ironic, isn't it," said Jenny, "that what was a pacifist community is now a motorsports playground."

"To say the least," Hank offered. "And a damn shame, given the distinct ecosystem of the dunes. There are plenty of beaches in California that could support some controlled form of motorized recreation. But most of those shorelines are overlooked by expensive homes, so it ain't likely."

"But the town of Oceano has stayed largely the same," Pearl said. "We call it a fishy little sleeping village."

Jenny was keen to know about Pearl's college studies, and what might be underway at the Avila pier. Hoping she sounded more inquisitive than interrogational.

"Well, the latest project, and probably my last one, is the Clam Study. In the spring we got a nice grant, funded by Scripps, the state and a group called EHRC, Environmental Human Rights Coalition, to study the rise and fall of the Pismo Clam. So we have to go through all the historical research, compare and contrast, yada-yada, study and assess the current status of the mollusk, and then come up with some recommendations for the future. No official title yet. My own working title is, "Remain Clam: Kelp is On the Way."

Jenny made a note to check out the EHRC, and asked Hank what role he played in the project.

"Uhh... guess I'm a lab assistant," he said. "But I could do with a title. How about Deputy, Offshore Operations Division? DOOD."

"You got it," Pearl said. "But you'll have to buy your own business cards."

"Unnecessary," he replied. "But I really could use a nice action suit, something that really blends in when you're in the water. Something really classy."

Pearl said, "I'm afraid I can see where this is going."

"Yeah," said Hank. "A real nice, class, action suit."

Moans. Jenny asked about the current status of the study, and when it might be complete.

"We've compiled all the historic and scientific data," Pearl said. "Some of the divers from the Fifties are still around, and a few Chumash elders, who we have scheduled for interviews. Then we'll sift and organize, form conclusions and hypotheses, figure out the graphics and stuff. We should have it done by fall, in time for the Clam Festival."

"By which time you will have another degree," Hank observed. "And you'll have to get a real job."

"One of us will. Maybe I'll run the surf shack and you can put that B.A. in English to work." At which they smiled at each other warmly, and broke into a Cracker song

How can I live without you,

If it means I gotta get a job...

Whereupon Jenny experienced some satisfaction in the knowledge that of these two bright, attractive young people, at least the blonde couldn't sing a lick. And noted her added good fortune that they were not in a karaoke bar. Pearl, of course, had the voice of an angel.

The calamari and shrimp appetizers had disappeared, and enough beer and wine to suit the occasion of a working meet. Jenny's notes included sufficient thumbnail data on the Pismo Clam. It's predators, besides man and sea otters, included seagulls, crabs, manta rays and sharks; that their lifespan ranged from 20 to 50 years, that like oysters they can create pearls, and that at maturity they measure from four to seven inches. And that clamming on the beach requires a fishing license; the limit is ten, which must be at least 4.5 inches, and undersized clams must be reburied.

The old days had long been gone away. "Nobody likes to pay for other people's mistakes," Pearl said. "But in this case it comes with the territory. And it's cumulative, because we're dealing with the effects of errors made by generations long past, plus the ones people keep adding. Now we've got this herbicide called Atrazine, which affects animals' hormonal systems."

"Affects them how?" Jenny asked.

"It turns testosterone into estrogen. Male frogs are turning into females, they can make babies. So if weed killer is getting down to the frogs, it's in the water table, and the ocean. Which means it's in the crops, and in the food. And ultimately in us."

"You mean I could have your baby?" asked Hank. The women regarded him sternly.

Pearl noted that this acceleration of types and amounts of chemical pollution and the rising temperature of the ocean was not a healthy forecast. The earth will remain a self-cleaning organism only to a certain point, she asserted. A point uncertain, but one drawing ever nearer. A thoughtful silence enveloped the table.

Jenny's thoughts returned to the Varian brothers, who had been working with electromagnetic radiation seventy years ago, just beyond these dunes. As mystics and artists moved through them. A curious admixture of physics and philosophy. Then she clicked back to the present. "Do either of you know an old guy named Dugan Byrnes?"

Part Two

"We live subject to the moment according to cycles of light and dark, of weeks and months. Our bodies have tides, and flow with measurable impulses of electric magnetism. It may be that we live strung like our telegraph wires in fields of waves of all kinds and lengths, waves we can see and hear and waves we cannot, and the life we feel, the animacy, is what is shaken through us by these waves..."

The Waterworks
– E. L. Doctorow

Seven

Only a few couples and families occupied the end of the pier, with no epic sunset in the prospect. Dugan stood with his back to the sea, collar up against the onshore wind and watched the sunlight fade on the rolling tan hills across the highway. His pet names for this favorite terminus of planks and pilings alternated to match his mood; Point Reflection… Resignation… Exclamation Point!

Or Point Expiration. His choice of a place to die, should he be given one, had long been made. No better spot than right here on the last bench west, waiting for the glory train after a few beers at Harry's, fish tacos and another beer at the Cool Cat, and a slow shuffle down the pier. Cue the spectacular sunset, perhaps a last cosmic wink of the green flash, and the final surprise. To be discontinued… Splash.

His terms of agreement with mortality had been signed way back in Korea, during the winter of the Chinese advance across the Yalu River. A cyclorama of grayed whiteness shrouded the entire landscape; the Chinese troops in hooded white canvas uniforms emerged from the vapors, only their blazing weapons visible. At first many of them fell under fire, their blood pooling red to black in the snow. But more came, and still more.

With a curious calmness, he figured this might be it; just get shot and drain away into the cold powder, or freeze to death, or both. Big fuckin' deal. Rather be in Philadelphia, but bring it. Hope the ones who picked this fight get theirs properly, like trying to stuff their intestines back in with their hands, their friends and family in attendance.

Whereupon the order came to withdraw, and with it a strange metallic aftertaste of disappointment. As if he'd been cheated from death, by death. Had got himself ready to go, sign the check, pay the piper, quit the scene. But was denied, the offer of his life ignored. Any notion of shame at American soldiers in retreat did not occur to him. But getting his mind right to close the deal, then being rejected by the reaper, worked a turning point in Dugan's changing perceptions. He was a different man, in ways as yet unclear.

But, as he would admit, the better part of the ensuing decades had been prodigiously rewarding, in terms of learning, friends and true adventure, though not financial security. And until the death of his wife Grace fifteen years ago, he could say with conviction, "It's all good." Most of it leastways.

. . .

"Korea!?" Henry said. "Jesus, that was sixty years ago! You sign up in grade school?" "I was almost sixteen," Dugan replied, "but I was a big kid, had a beard. My friend Chick Singer made up the bogus birth certificate and I sailed right in. I was pretty pissed off when my brother got killed over there."

"You had a friend named Chick Singer?"

"His real name was Gary. We all had nicknames, being cool guys and all. My favorite was Salvatore Vendetti.

"That was his nickname?"

"No, his real one. His nickname was Sonny Lemontina."

"What was yours?"

"Never got one that stuck. A few girls called me Doogle, and once in a while someone would call me Noggin. Never knew if it was a reference to my refined intelligence or for taking numerous blows to the skull. Anyway, what have we on the new handles, my friend?"

"We're now pouring a Ninkasi Tricerahops, a double IPA, so where the Tri comes from who knows, except for the dinosaur pun. It's eight-point-eight alcohol, with a high caramel front end, a touch of light citrus on the tongue, think like mango, maybe a little grapefruit, bit of vanilla, and a blend of deep mahogany and Corinthian leather in the finish."

"That was eloquent, Henry. I will forgive your omission of the IBU and the original gravity."

"The International Bitterness Unit is one hundred, and the original gravity is ten-eighty."

"You are the best fucking bartender in the world."

On the jukebox, James Taylor was thinking about women and glasses of beer. Dugan was drinking a pleasant brew from Eugene, Oregon, and looking at a handsome woman on the other side of the horseshoe bar. A new face, but somehow familiar. Lovely auburn hair. Two guys at the end were playing Shrubbies, after Dubya, a game assigning the best nickname to the politicians holding forth on the TV news channel, always on without audio. "How about him, John McCain?"

"Mission Creep."

"Oww..., that's good." They watched the puffy visage on the monitor for a few more seconds. "It's like looking into the jowls of death."

The screen then presented Lindsey Graham ("Lesley Reptile") and Mitch McConnell ("Sniveling Turtle"), followed by the burnished mug of John Boehner. "The Brown Bummer," said one. "Not bad," from the other. "But I like The Grim Weeper. Another contender was the Sour Kraut. He reminds me of a drunk back in our neighborhood bar in Philly. He was such a whiner that after awhile nobody would talk to him; just sat at the bar mumbling to himself. Had that same beady-eyed, prune-face look."

The screen switched to Barack Obama at a lectern. "The Black Bummer," said the first. "Not being racist or anything. I mean the poor bastard had some good ideas, but the mouthbreathers shut him down at every turn. Look at the poor guy, a few years ago he looked like Will Smith. Now he looks like Morgan Freeman."

Dugan raised his glass and voice to the players. "I cast a vote for Mission Creep, gentlemen. That is spot on and possibly brilliant. Have you a matching moniker for his vice-presidential running mate, the lovely governess of Alaska?"

"Oh, there were many. I liked Barbie Troll. Have you got one for the record?"

"I do," replied Dugan. "How about Veronica Honky?"

"Yes!" they cried in unison, and lifted their glasses. "Cheers!" The trio also agreed on the forthcoming entertainment prospects of the Republican presidential nominating process. Another carnival sideshow of runaway conflation, sure to get all the rubes worked up. Political slapstick overcast by a gray cloud of sorrow for the species. Dugan was reminded of poet Brendan Kenelley's comment on the debit side of Irish history, "the legacy of prejudices, hatreds, clichés and an impressive supply of apparently invincible ignorance."

Next on the TV soapbox was a guy who looked like he'd just stepped out of a Scorsese movie. "Who's the guy with the Tony Curtis collar?" Dugan asked. "He looks like a televangelist, or a pimp." A distinction without a difference.

"That's the governor of Texas. He could be our next president." To which Dugan could formulate no reply, found himself in the completely unfamiliar realm of speechlessness. Stupefied.

· · ·

Jack Padilla had left a phone message – *gone to Mexico, family business, gotta postpone the research mission, we'll reschedule.* Draining his beer, Dugan noticed that the woman across the bar was now looking more familiar, and a bit lovelier. The potential for a religious experience on a Sunday evening at Harry's was not outside the realm of possibility, a realm that grew more expansive with time. Dugan asked Henry to inquire if the lady might like a drink. She smiled and waved, he moved.

"I didn't think you remembered me," she said. Ahh, the owner of Shirley the retriever on the beach. "But surely I do," he replied. "You look a bit different without the wool cap."

"Did you locate your fishing boat?"

"Oh it wasn't mine, something was just wrong with its movement. I thought you might have seen it. I was looking for a witness."

"Like it was in distress?"

"No, it looked fine, shipshape as they say, except it was going backwards."

"That's unusual."

"Indeed. And it kept going backwards until it was out of sight, and seems I'm the only one who saw it."

"Was that the one the Coast Guard towed in last week?"

"That seems quite likely, by the description I got. But I haven't seen the ship, it disappeared the same day. Have you heard about it?"

"Yes, and I may have a lead for you," she said. "My ex-husband works at the boat house at Vandenberg. He said it showed up there and was cordoned off and inspected by a crew he didn't recognize. A couple days later they put it on a trailer and took it to some state impound yard in Lompoc."

"So the feds are in the game, or it wouldn't go through an air force base. That was just last week. Wonder if it's still there." He wondered at yet another strange turn in this evolving narrative. He also wondered if she had really emphasized the *ex* in ex-husband.

"Do you live in Pismo?" he asked warmly.

"I'm damn near a native. My folks lived just over the ridge in the valley, and they did okay even in the depression. They had 80 acres, good wells. And even when the clams were gone the fishing was still good, and people still ate vegetables and beef, chickens, game birds. My brother and I actually had a wonderful childhood."

"He still in the neighborhood?"

"No..., he didn't come back from Vietnam. I mean, not even in a box, so he may still be alive somewhere. I picture him on a Greek island, with a small sloop and a rich girlfriend."

"Sounds like the old guy who flees the assisted-living home and his family, saying he wants to die with dignity. Then he sends them a card with a picture of himself with a naked 20-year-old Samoan girl, which reads '… and Dignity says hello too.'"

She had a good warm laugh. "I'm Gina," she said. "Dugan, pleased to meet you. Have you had dinner? I was going to grill some scallops and make a salad, maybe a glass of Edna Valley pinot gris?"

"You're talking my language, sailor. Next you'll tell me about the hot tub and breathtaking ocean views."

"Got them too," he smiled. She wasn't reminded of Sean Connery.

The radio stayed on full-time at his place, tuned to either NPR or KPIG; not loud enough to annoy the neighbors, but sufficient volume to give amateur thieves a second thought. Tonight it was playing a rocker by the late John "Juke" Logan

She was young and wired, he was old and tired,
But they went on just the same,
They was way out west, they did their best
Just to scandalize their names.

Gina and Dugan did the old folks boogie on the deck. "I'm not all that young," she said.

"Old enough to vote, I trust."

"And then some."

"And sense enough to not vote Republican?"

"Likewise," she said. Dugan had forgotten about the wine, and dinner, and hoped she had as well. When the song ended they kissed, and nuzzled, and took off their clothes as the sun fell away. The tub had also evaporated from their collective thoughts, but, for Dugan at least, the view was breathtaking.

Eight

Former army Private First Class Byrnes had seen some unusual marine activity in his time with the federal armed forces, among both the enlisted grunts and officers. The oddball ratio among marines may have been higher than the other branches, but all forms of military service often promoted a sense of privilege well out of proportion to the requirements of the job.

"The anger management issue is more prevalent in the marines," said Henry, who spoke from experience. "A lot of those guys are pissed off when they go in, and then they're encouraged to take it up a few notches. And some of them eventually flip out, usually after they're discharged, when the enemy is harder to identify. Unfortunate."

Dugan was well aware that mood modulation could be key to one's survival in the world of rough-and-tumble, and that he may have lucked out with only a half measure of the traditionally short-fused Irish temperament. The other half of his ethnic genome, the British side, with its jolly good, carry on, all's well and Bob's-your-uncle attitude, tended to mollify the violent impulses and usually keep him out of jail or the emergency room. Most of the time. Marines had been known to flip his switch. More than one friend had noted his habit of coming unhinged at the least opportune times. Genuine white-hot rage, he would assert, is immune to management.

In the morning, when Gina left after coffee, croissants and warm, fuzzy feelings, he checked out the old Ducati and rolled it out for a ride to Lompoc. No real expectations, take a nice ride, see if he could find the boat and check it out. And it took only a few friendly questions at the first tackle shop to locate the yard and roll in at midday. Almost too easy.

He recognized the Hatteras right away, a white flying bridge peeking above a sea of trailers, motorhomes and campers. The gate was open, a new Audi S5 parked next to the boat. Someone was aboard. Dugan walked past the stern, noticing a fit-looking middle-aged man working on something on the deck. *Jokers Mild, Marina del Ray,* and on the transom a sticker with the familiar round logo. United States Marine Corps, surrounding a globe with outlines of North and South America, bisected by an anchor, topped by an eagle with spread wings holding in its beak a banner, "Semper Fidelis," the motto first used by the Irish Brigade in France in 1691. Always faithful or not, looked like this marine had been landed. The prop was deformed.

He turned back. "Hello aboard!" A head appeared above the gunwale. "Yes?"

"I just noticed the new addition to the yard," Dugan said. "Putting her up for the season?"

"Uh…, no, just temporary storage, and a little clean-up. In fact, I think she may go up for sale pretty soon." Aussie accent. "You're not the owner?"

"No, just helping getting her ready. Had some electrical issues."

"You need a hand?"

"Well…, I gotta lower this generator down. It's on the winch, but if you don't mind, maybe just steady it to keep it off the side of the boat." With the unit on the ground, the man came down the sea ladder and dropped the last few feet. "Thanks, mate," extending a hand. "That could have been a tussle with this rig up on a trailer. I'm Kev."

"Dugan, glad to help. You know, I saw a boat that looked like this a week ago, just off Pismo."

"When it was being towed in?"

"No, when it was going out." At which the friendliness factor seemed to drop a few notches. "You from the FBI?"

"No, just a concerned citizen. When you see a boat going out to sea backwards, that gets your attention."

"You saw it! They didn't believe us, man. Questioned us for three fuckin' hours, the assholes. Then said we didn't want to talk to anyone about it, especially the media. What a bunch of fuckwits. Matter of national security. Bullshit. Impounded the boat for ten days."

"Can you tell me what happened?"

"This guy from the east coast charters the boat for three days, paid cash Pete said, and he comes aboard in Pismo. Says his name's Marty, a real dickhead, has a big gear bag. Says he just wants to catch a marlin, has a bet with some buddies in New Jersey. So we're out most of the day, he gets a couple hits but loses 'em. He gets more pissed by the hour, throwing beer bottles over the side."

"Pete's the captain?"

"Yeah, and he wants to tell the guy to fuck off. But this jerk insists we stay overnight in Pismo and go back out the next day. So we drop anchor and Pete goes to call Debbie, his girlfriend, to come out in the Zodiac and pick us up. But the radio is out, so he tries his cell phone. Nothing. My cell won't work either, and the client is passed out on a bunk in the forward cabin.

"So Pete decides to weigh anchor and move in by the pier and go ashore in the dinghy. But the engine won't start, we have no electrical power anywhere. And that's when we started to move."

"Backwards."

"True story, mate. Slowly at first, we thought it was just a groundswell or a weird tidal thing. Then, as the speed went up, that we might be caught in some kind of earthquake or tsunami phenomenon. But the sea was calm, and the rate stabilized, maybe seven or eight knots. So we got ready to deploy the dinghy and wake up Marty the dickhead. We were being towed."

"By what?"

"No idea. A submarine? We couldn't see a line, nothing broke the surface. It was supremely weird, mate. Pete finally got the generator started and it ran for ten seconds, then quit. Nothing electrical worked, not even the flashlights. By then it was nightfall, and we got flares ready, but never saw another ship. Then, about three a.m., we stopped. We drifted southwest, until just before sunrise."

"Then what happened?"

"Okay, you won't believe this. The feds didn't, and I've been questioning my own bloody sanity ever since. There was a slight tug at the stern and we started moving again. I went to the wheel and Pete was below, checking all the electrics again. Then out comes Marty, looking all crazed, and hollers what the fuck is going on, yelling and shit, and I say we're being towed out to sea, maybe by a Russian sub. "By now the ocean was coming up and I'm tending the rudder so we don't get sideways." Marty is screaming, 'Come on you motherfuckers! I'll kill you commie bastards!'

"So I turn to look, the gear bag is open on the deck and he's holding a Thompson submachine gun! He staggers to the stern, gets off maybe a dozen rounds into the water, and disappears."

"What do you mean, like vanishes?"

"Exactly, mate. That dude was Hoovered off the deck, man. It was like one of those canisters in the vacuum tube, like in the old stores. Thwop! He was gone."

"What about the Thompson?"

"Took it with him."

Kev went on to recount how Pete had come through the hatch wielding a 12-inch Crescent wrench, thinking they were under attack by pirates. How they again went adrift, spent another night at sea drinking their ex-client's beer and speculating on their bizarre situation. The captain thought Kev might have had an acid flashback, but shit, the Jersey guy was gone. Mid-morning the next day the Coast Guard cutter arrived and towed them back to Pismo. The feds confiscated the gear bag and took them both to Vandenberg Air Force Base for questioning. Separately. Both were asked if they had been using hallucinogenic drugs, and firmly invited to please check in if they planned to leave the state any time soon.

Dugan thanked him for the information, pledged to keep it confidential, and pointed Grazia, his trusty Italian V-twin, toward home. Riding the Ducati always helped clarify the confusions of reality, and the unfolding costume dramas of the cosmos. But this scenario was well out there in the ether, beyond the outlines of any concepts or perceptions he could recall. Science fiction come true? Who could be writing this script? What strange creatures were ready to take the stage?

At home by noon, he indulged in a normally eventide libation, Jameson on the rocks with a splash of coffee. One message on the machine, from Padilla. *Hey, I'm back, come for dinner tonight, bring the good wine.*

Nine

Gloria answered the door. Dugan had to wonder if a woman could be more aptly named. Jack's wife, whose granny had told her she was part Cherokee, looked more like a Scandinavian princess. One of those statuesque beauties who in earlier times had sent the Vikings off to sea, that they might return with sweets and cute shoes. She always made his neurons go all squirmy.

"Hi, sweetcakes," she said. "We hoped you could make it. And that you would bring a bottle of…"

"Wild Horse pinot noir," he said, offering the wine and an embrace, which he always held a beat too long.

"Oooh, lovely. Jack's in the shop. We're having shrimp tacos with asparagus risotto. Twenty minutes."

He found his host in the garage at the bow of a 24-foot panga boat, with a rivet gun in one hand an a beer in the other. "Hey, get yourself a beer. The Mexicans know how to build these things well enough, but they don't put much effort into maintenance."

"Too busy with the Zen, no doubt. How was Mexico?"

"Same problem, lack of maintenance. My uncle was having some issues with the local drug dealers, but we took care of it. Had to liberate this boat, since they had no more use for it."

"I won't ask how."

"Good. They won't be causing more problems, but they'll just be replaced." "So what's going on?"

"We can talk after dinner, which I have to go help with. First I want you to read something I printed from the Internet," handing him a page. "Made me think of the report you saw in the Scripps guy's room."

Dugan took the stool at the workbench, set the bottle of Barrel-house IPA, and read:

45

It is well established that the function and metabolism of the human body is an electrochemical system. Modern medicine is preoccupied with studying, analyzing and treating mainly the chemical side of the equation. For the most part, the electrical half of human systems has been completely ignored. Physicians use several of the body's electrical systems for diagnosis (e.g., EKG, EEG, EMG and MEGs), though even fewer uses of the electromagnetics are found for therapeutics (e.g., cardiac pacemakers, defibrillators, TENs devices, bone healing instruments).

Physiology reveals that most of the body's natural chemicals are released by an electrical signal or an electrochemical reaction. Can these same chemicals be released by applying an external electrical signal? Can different EM parameters stimulate different chemical systems? Simply stated, can externally applied bioelectromagnetic fields influence cell and organismal behavior and expression?

The answer is a clear, resounding, and unequivocal, YES! Electromagnetic energy fields, which include energies in the ranges of microwaves, radio-frequencies, the visible light spectrum, ELF and even acoustic frequencies, have been shown to profoundly impact every facet of biological regulation. Specific frequencies and patterns of electromagnetic radiation regulate:

1. *cell division;*
2. *gene regulation;*
3. *DNA, RNA and protein synthesis;*
4. *protein conformation and function;*
5. *morphogenesis;*
6. *regeneration;*
7. *ion transport and regulation through cell membranes;*
8. *nerve conduction and growth.*

The text was credited to Prof. Dr. Charles McWilliams, PanAmerican School of Natural Medicine, 2009, and followed by a footnote:

*Morphogenetic responses may be induced in organisms by
hormones, by environmental chemicals ranging from substances
produced by other organisms to toxic chemicals or radionuclides
released as pollutants, and other plants, or by mechanical stresses
induced by spatial patterning of the cells.*

· · ·

Dugan had no clue on the validity of the science, but it sounded reasonable. Jack always seemed to pull this stuff out of the air. While
he looked like the love child of Jack Palance and Charles Bronson,
a disturbing visual, Padilla had the intellectual curiosity of a serious
academic. And he could rebuild any engine ever made. An uncommon synthesis. The bastard was even pretty good on guitar.

Dugan emptied the beer and headed for the house. On the wall
by the door hung a painting he had never noticed. The plain black
frame had an engraved brass plaque at the bottom: *Henry Ford Looks
at the American Indian.* The scene, reminiscent of Norman Rockwell's
style with a harder edge, pictured Henry Ford at a large desk, the
industrial landscape of the River Rouge factory visible through the
window behind him. Ford's hands are lifted above the desk, palms
up, as if emphasizing a point to the native American seated across
from him.

The Indian, in traditional Sioux garb, sits erect with his right
hand raised, palm forward, in the traditional gesture of greeting. His
left arm, however, remains on the arm of the chair, palm up and fist
clenched, but for the middle finger, which is distinctly erect. And just
below the frame, a printed card:

*"Any man who thinks he can be happy and prosperous by letting the
American government take care of him better take a closer look at
the American Indian."*

– Henry Ford

···

At dinner the conversation turned on the drought dragging on toward five years, the possibility of a local desalination plant, and rumors of wind and/or wave energy projects offshore. Change was blowin' in the wind, plenty of questions but not many answers.

Dugan, ever the polite guest, asked Gloria about her teaching job in Santa Maria, but she was circumspect. "It's a daily challenge," she said. "Most of those kids don't have very good prospects." The agricultural basin a few miles to the south, developed by oilman Allan Hancock in the thirties, was now commonly referred to as North Tijuana. Rarely a day passed without a stabbing, drug bust, shooting or heist. Maybe Mexico's hold on California had never been severed.

"What say we sweep Avila and Pismo tomorrow," Jack said. "Then I can just leave the panga at your place, since I got no room for it right now."

"You brought a boat back from Mexico," Gloria asked, "so you could store it at his house?"

"Not a problem," said Dugan. "Got an empty carport. The dune buggy is on extended loan to my sister's kid in Portland. He's in high school, I figured it might help him get laid."

That got him the schoolmarm frown, half serious. As they cleared the table, he and Jack outlined a rough plan to scan a few miles of coastline and just have a look-see. First-hand data always trumped second-hand reports, and it was a good excuse to get out on the water.

"I'll load up the gear tonight, pick you up first thing in the morning," Jack said. "Beer and sandwiches on you."

"Cool deal. Where did you find the Henry Ford portrait in the shop?"

"That was done by a guy who worked at the casino, used to do portraits of guests. Brilliant cat, Arapaho, lived in a trailer out back. Anyway, I rebuilt a motorcycle engine for him and he was broke, so I took the painting in trade."

"You gonna tell me it was an Indian engine?"

"That would be good, eh? No, in fact it was a Velocette single. Neat engine."

"I like the detail in the painting, and you have to take a closer look to notice the political message."

"Yeah, Jake held Ford in some contempt. Said he took the last wrong turn, steered the country away from the tradition of craftsmanship and into large scale industrialization. That and generally acting like just another mick bigot."

"Sure, and do we not produce some of the world's finest?," Dugan replied in his Barry Fitzgerald brogue.

"Jake Simmons was his so-called Christian name. He said it was the custom in his tribe that young men would choose their own tribal names when they came of age."

"What was his?"

"Fuck Me Running."

Ten

Spence was taking his parting look at the ocean from the hotel patio when he noticed two men in a panga boat just offshore. His interview with Jenny had been pleasant, though he'd had little to contribute to her story. Three days of diving had turned up nothing in the water, beyond a curious row of evenly spaced bowls in the sand, running parallel to the pier. He'd taken photos and packaged a few samples of the sand to take back to the lab.

Nor had Jenny gathered any noteworthy facts from Pearl and Hank, though the local history was intriguing and it seemed she'd made new friends. She had swapped messages with Byrnes, who said he was gone on a scouting expedition and would get back to her in a couple days. The possibility of a missed deadline loomed.

Spence had hoped to see Pearl again before heading home, but no luck. For the moment the panga occupied his attention, as it moved slowly south about 75 yards from the beach. Retrieving the field glasses from his pack, he brought the craft into focus. At the tiller he could see the old guy from the bar, Byrnes, who trailed something under water attached to a jointed metal rod. At the bow stood a man in a wetsuit, with a mask and snorkel, headgear with a GoPro camera attached, and holding a pistol-shaped instrument that looked like an automotive timing gun.

Byrnes slowed the engine as the other man moved to the center and slipped over the side. In his free hand was a line attached to the transom, and as the engine picked up he was towed along behind, face down. The pair maintained a slow pace following the arc of the shore, pausing off Oceano where the snorkeler climbed back aboard, and they came about toward Pismo.

Spence recalled how inquisitive the old man had been, and that Jenny had mentioned his interest when she met him in the bar.

Could this person be with some government agency? Was he under surveillance? Who are those guys?

With a travel day left before he was due back in La Jolla, Spence decided another night in Pismo was in order. He wondered if Byrnes had learned anything about the backwards fishing boat, and what he might be looking for in the bay. Why would anyone be interested in his research, when he didn't even know any details himself? And why wouldn't Jenny even know what she was looking for, since her assignment editor must have had some reason to send her?

The questions bumped into one another in his head until he got back to the room. Where he opened the door to find two men in suits, sitting on the bed playing blackjack. They looked like twins. At his entrance they both looked up and said, in unison, "Spencer Nolan?"

. . .

Pearl stared out the window of the lab, watching the ocean get itself ready for bed. A triangulate of pelicans swept past. She wondered which creatures actually slept, or just took quick naps, and how the sharks and whales could doze in motion. Then her own submerged database opened an old undergraduate file: As conscious breathers, dolphins have to surface, but they have the ability to rest one side of the brain at a time. Some evidence suggests that sharks, like the Great White, which must take oxygen from water passing through their gills, have an automatic pilot mechanism in the spine. So they can sleep and swim at the same time.

She longed to swim with them, to leap and dive and listen to their songs. Her mother said she had been born in the ocean, in a cove on St. Thomas, and that at birth she glowed iridescent, like a pearl. That she was *del oceano,* of the ocean. And now lived in a town of the same name. Coincidence? Pearl took little offense that her nickname had been appropriated by a screenwriter as the name of a pirate ship. She vowed to try free diving when her degree was final.

When her first college boyfriend, the artist Akbar Johnson, titled her portrait "Black Pearl," the nickname stuck like beach tar. She had posed for his figure studies class, as a liberated woman who could use the money, but the finished painting caused quite a stir at the school. She was shown rising from the surf, full frontal, her hips and breasts rather enhanced she thought, raising a hand to clear the hair from her eyes, also a bit too green. Shiny droplets of water descended from her shoulders, nipples, stomach and thighs, and her black bush glistened with reflected highlights, as if it were lighted from within. The classroom fell silent for what seemed a long time, when, approaching awkwardness, the silence took a left turn without signaling, and one by one the male students began to applaud, followed reluctantly by the females.

It was an arresting image. Akbar called the style Neoclassic Photorealism. One girl called it Goya does Playboy. A guy asked Akbar if he would make prints for sale. Another if he might do a matching piece of Pearl walking into the ocean, and offer the prints as matching panels.

At first she wondered if the blushing she felt actually altered her skin color, which Akbar called milk chocolate. But the overriding sensation, the bolt of enlightenment that shifted her own self image dramatically, was the realization that this was how most men saw her. Not as a sex object necessarily, (better than a subject she liked to say), that was a given. But rather as an idealized symbol of the primal feminine force in nature; strong, unafraid, rooted in organic harmony with the planet. Wet. And sexy. Alright, she thought. I can live with that.

A computer chime brought her back to present tense reality, in the form of an email from Jenny, asking if when a draft of the clam study was ready could she have a copy for reference. And if she and Hank could come to her place for dinner when their schedules allowed. She replied yes on both counts, thanking Jenny for the reminder that it was time to get back to work. At issue was the license renewal application for the Diablo Canyon nuclear power plant, and what kinds of damage to marine life were the result of a cooling system that sucked in 2.5 billion gallons of seawater a day, which carried an unknown number of animal larvae, and returned it to the ocean 20 degrees warmer.

The effect on the localized clam population over 33 years would be an informed guess at best. Few general studies had been done, none comparing the impacts to adjacent segments of the coastline. The data from Pacific Gas and Electric was expectedly sparse and inconclusive, and the California Coastal Commission had shown little interest in the subject. The Environmental Protection Agency had a team doing similar research on the east coast, but chose not to share any information until the project was completed.

Pearl entertained the notion that the results of the Cal Poly study were going to attract plenty of attention, that they would be peer-reviewed extensively before publication, and would likely leave more than a few people pissed off. Their problem.

She hankered for a shrimp quesadilla and a beer.

• • •

Hank logged the last of the day's receipts for the surf shop, which like the waves and afternoon temperatures were down. He wondered if the strange weather was affecting our nuclear testing. He'd read that the nation's 4500 nuclear weapons, stationed strategically around the country, were in need of upgrades and replacements. The refurb would take about ten years and cost around $300 billion. But you can't be too safe.

Closing the plywood overhead door/awning he noticed the hand-lettering in the upper corner, likely inked before he was born.

HAYDUKE LIVES! Just the night before, over beers with some other grousing surfers at the Shell Cafe, the subject had come up. Where's the Monkey Wrench Gang, now that we really need them? Did the spirit die with Ed Abbey? WTF?

"Safety third," said one. "But you can hardly blow up a nuclear power plant."

"Not helpful," Hank agreed. "That one will have to be phased out, but it could probably be crippled without harming anyone. Force it to shut down."

"Before this conspiracy goes further," another said, "we should take the conversation elsewhere. Who knows who might be listening these days."

While the assembled malcontents made no plans for any widespread eco-sabotage, the talk stirred Hank's seasonal notion of a sabbatical in the desert. The old ocean, H2No. Maybe the sea is too much with us, late and soon. Get away to the red rocks, dry heat and mystical vistas afloat in the blazing sunsets. Soon as Pearl could get some time off, and he changed the oil in the van. Found someone to run the shop for awhile, and so forth.

Eleven

Jack and Dugan occupied a corner table at Harry's, otherwise all but empty at mid-afternoon. Each stared at the murky video on the laptop screen, sipping respectively a Figueroa Mountain Stagecoach Stout and a Firestone Double Jack IPA. The satellite radio streamed John Prine

> ... we lost Davy in the Korean war, and I still don't know what for,
> don't matter anymore. Ya' know that old trees just grow stronger,
> and old rivers grow wilder every day.
> Old people just grow lonesome, waiting for someone to say,
> "Hello in there, hello."

"None of this footage shows much of anything," Jack said. "Except for those hummocks along the pier, there's squat. And I didn't get any visuals, beyond the usual trash and what looked like the top of a '36 Chevy."

"The sonar gun didn't show anything on the screen, and it went blank for a few seconds, like it lost power. But there was something from the trailing camera that I can't make out, and it was there on the way down and back. Here, take a look."

Jack bent closer to the screen. The object maintained position at the top of the frame, just below the surface, fifty or sixty feet astern and barely visible. It looked like five small balloons in V formation, with a dark object in the middle.

"What the hell is that?" he asked. "Looks like it was following us."

"So it would appear. The distance stays about the same, but with the wide angle lens and the water... can't get a fix on it."

"Radio controlled maybe?"

"S'pose it's possible, but it doesn't look like anything mechanical. The shape keeps changing slightly."

Henry joined them, absent any patrons at the bar. "I'll have to caution you gentlemen that we don't allow customers to bring their own porn."

"Have a look at this, Henry," Dugan said, turning the screen. "What do you make of that object in the top left corner?"

"Looks like a little paper triangle, with polka dots, as seen from the bottom of the aquarium. What is it?"

"We can't tell. But it seemed to be tailing us in the bay."

"You might want to show it to Mark, the owner's son-in-law. He's real good at video stuff, might could enlarge the image. He's got a studio right next door in the hotel.

"Speaking of tails," Henry said, "there were a couple feds in here last night."

"Feds, like what… FBI?" Dugan asked.

"No these guys looked collegiate, not like jarnecks. I'd guess maybe ATF or DEA."

"Jarnecks?" asked Jack.

"Yeah, you know, not ex-marines necessarily. Just those guys with necks wider than their head. They tend to be independent contractors, and they don't wear suits."

"They say what they wanted?" Dugan inquired.

"Not specifically. But they did ask about you."

"Really?"

"Asked if I knew you, had I seen you lately, whether you were a private detective."

"What did you tell them?"

"Well, you know, I had to have a little fun with 'em. Said that even though you'd long been a regular customer, nobody really knew much about you. That it was rumored you were special ops in 'Nam, that you had a role in the Watergate investigation, and that one rumor was you once worked as a personal astrologer for Nancy Reagan. I think they got a little suspicious when I related the scuttlebutt that you had actually been undercover in the Pakistan compound when they got bin Laden."

"So you were just being truthful," Byrnes said.

"Exactly," Henry smiled. "I'll get you Mark's phone number. You might be able to catch him in the office today."

"I can see why he's your favorite bartender," Jack said when Henry returned to the bar. "Why in the hell would any feds be snooping around about you?"

"Good question. And one that has now been added to the list. Maybe we're getting too close to something they don't want us to know."

"What do you think they know?"

"Obviously not much if they're down to me."

"Well, if you want to take the underwater surveillance up several notches, you should talk to Pearl over at the Poly pier. They have those little remote-control submarines with much better cameras than we have."

"Can you set that up?"

"Lemme talk to Hank, her boyfriend, he's a surfing buddy. Reckon he could at least make the introduction, then it would be up to you."

Henry returned with Mark's number. Jack said he'd talk to Hank and be in touch about meeting with Pearl. "Why don't we go next door and see if Mark is in first?" Dugan said. "Maybe we can still salvage something from this video."

• • •

"Yes, that's me," Spence replied, as the two men in suits rose from the bed. They looked like Mormons. "Who the hell are you?"

"Sorry for the intrusion, Mr. Nolan," said one. "I'm Brian Stargell and this is Glen Handler. We're with the federal government, investigating some curious activities here on the coast. We were put in touch with Scripps regarding your research, and they were cooperative in assisting with our inquiry."

"And they gave you permission to break into my room?"

"Well," said Glen, "more or less. We have a working agreement with them when issues of national security are involved."

"And you think I'm a threat to national security?"

"Not exactly," Brian replied. "But your assignment has created some… let's say outside interest that is a matter of concern."

"Outside interest from… Wait a minute, can I see some ID?"

"Of course," said Handler, who produced a photo ID with an embossed logo of the DEA. Stargell offered a similar card, identifying him as an employee of the Bureau of Alcohol, Tobacco and Firearms. The ATF acronym always reminded Spence to check his car's automatic transmission fluid.

"What the hell does oceanography have to do with drugs or weapons?" he asked.

"Well," Handler replied, "we can't discuss our investigation, but rest assured that you are under no suspicion. We do have something to show you, however, that may help explain the situation." At which the other man withdrew a laptop from his shoulder bag, opened it on the desk and tapped the touch-pad.

A video image of the hotel room materialized on the screen. A surveillance camera. Spence glanced up at the overhead light fixture, then back at the screen, which showed a dateline of two days ago, and a digital clock, 7:42:18, 19, 20… Then a shadow appears on the wall, passes over his bicycle, and approaches the desk. The intruder enters the frame, a man wearing a leather jacket and baseball cap. With a pocketknife he lifts the cover of a manila envelope, studies it briefly, then does likewise with the adjacent screen of his laptop, reads the page and closes the screen with the knife's handle. The figure then withdraws, followed by the click of a closing door.

"Do you recognize that man?" asked Stargell.

Spence found himself temporarily dumbstruck. Obviously it was the old guy from the bar, Byrnes, who had seemed anything but a criminal. And he hadn't stolen anything, so it didn't seem necessary to give him up to the feds. "I'm not sure," he said.

"His name is Dugan Byrnes," said Handler. "We have information that you met him at Harry's Bar the other day."

"You know what, that's right. We had a beer the day I arrived. Interesting guy. Is he a drug smuggler?"

"Have you heard from him since then?" asked Stargell.

"Nope. And I can't imagine why he'd be in my room."

"That's what we'd like to know," Handler said. "We'd appreciate hearing from you if he does get in touch."

With that they left, and Spence had only more puzzlements. The agents hadn't mentioned the backwards boat, or Jenny, or Pearl. Had he been under surveillance since he arrived in Pismo, and if so at whose request? And they even have a mole at Harry's?! What the hell is everyone looking for? He felt this might be a good time to get back to San Diego, before things could get more weird. Then his thoughts turned to Pearl, and he felt better.

Someone in the next room cranked up the stereo, and the sounds of Little Feat filled the walls:

You've got to put on your sailin' shoes
Put on your sailing shoes
Everyone will start to cheer
When you put on your sailin' shoes

Twelve

Mark Stratton worked the front desk part-time in the old Pismo Beach Hotel, which granted him an adjacent space for his video editing equipment, and a small apartment for he and his wife Brenda. A nice arrangement, since they were both going to school part-time, and her father not only owned the hotel, but had just bought Harry's Bar. News of the sale had caused some local consternation. Several biker clubs had informed the new proprietor that if he turned Harry's into a yuppie wine bar, his continued good health couldn't be guaranteed.

The two guys at the desk looked like they may have made one of the calls to his father-in-law. "Hi," said the oldest one. "You must be Mark."

"I am. What can I do for you gentlemen? We have a few vacancies."

It had not occurred to Dugan until now that he and Jack might be taken for a gay couple. "No, we're actually here for your video expertise. You come recommended by Henry, the world's best bartender."

"That's good to hear, Henry's a good guy. Do you want something shot or edited, or both?"

"No," Dugan said. "For now we just wanted to see if you could enhance some underwater footage we took the other day. There's an object that we can't make out. It may be a lost cause."

"Glad to give it a try. I charge fifty bucks an hour, but if it's something that just won't improve then there's no fee. I can take a look and let you know by tomorrow."

"Fair enough. The item in question is at the top of the frame, what looks like some small balloons in a V shape." Dugan handed him the disc with his phone number on it. Jack had to wonder if his old pal might not be getting a bit too obsessive about all this. Clearly something was afoot in the local waters, whether it was mammal, fish or mollusk, domestic or foreign, man-made or of cosmic origin, Dugan was growing ever more consumed. The presence of snooping feds added another disturbance factor. And he'd noticed a sheriff's deputy pausing to eyeball him when he towed the panga boat into town. Jack knew he could easily be taken for a Mexican drug smuggler by a nervous cop. Gloria had listened patiently as he recounted Dugan's tale of the backwards boat and the disappearing gunman. "I know his imagination can run pretty far ahead of his sensibility, especially when the whiskey goes to work," she said. "But that sounds like a scene from a science fiction movie."

"Yeah, but so did the thing about Hector Romero, and that came from a reliable source."

"Has he turned up anything on the identity of the shooter?" she asked. "Did he talk to the owner of the boat to get his side of the story? And how come we haven't heard about any of this stuff in the local media?"

"He hasn't said any more about the boat, so I don't know. As for the lack of news, I'm beginning to think maybe some sort of gag order is at work. I should check with Stan at *The PennyPapers,* and the editor at *New Times.* Neither of them are corporate rags, and they both do some investigative reporting. If they're keeping a lid on it, then something big must be on the table."

"Are you sure Dugan's the only one obsessing?"

That gave Jack some pause. Wasn't really his mission, after all. She was right. But he and Dugan went back some ways, had survived a few scrapes that would have been far more painful, if not fatal, as solo enterprises, not to mention that business in Honduras with the Colombians. That would be a story for his grandchildren. He was in it now for good or ill, or at least till there was blood in the water.

···

Jenny dumped the last hay bale out of the truck and dragged it into the barn. Her editor at *Outside* had pushed the deadline a week, after which they would have to "re-think" the assignment. He was no more forthcoming on what she might be looking for, but to say a couple of their regular surfing contributors had been to Pismo in August, and reported wave action that was unlike anything they'd ever seen. Still not much to go on. She thought to check some outlets with shorter lead times; the story could be stale by the time a monthly magazine came out.

On the other hand she was caught up on ranch chores, the horses were happy, a warm fall evening was at hand and Pearl and Hank were due for dinner in an hour. She paused to savor the setting before heading to the bunkhouse for a shower.

With September drawing down, the annual heat wave had lifted but the brown hillsides remained parched. Jenny felt sorry for the ranchers with livestock, and farmers with thirsty crops like avocados, and miffed at the grape growers for demanding more water rights. But she still felt lucky to be in a beautiful place.

The absentee owners from Santa Barbara came up only four or five times a year, stayed a week at most, and left the routine maintenance of the spread up to Jenny. She was free to hire a temporary hand as the need arose – overgrown creek beds, wild boars, the occasional mountain lion or bear that might spook the horses – and her neighbors on either side were always willing to lend a hand, like country folk everywhere.

Once a year the landlords hosted a week-long gathering of friends and clients, (Frank and Monica handled respectively the financial and legal issues peculiar to show business people), which featured catered barbecues, live music, local wines and beers, and a three-day trail ride. The larger old barn was readied for guest horses, and Jenny was on-call full time to look after both the four- and two-legged guests, but was always welcome at the social activities.

The Trick or Treat Trail Ride was always around Halloween, which guaranteed both creative costumery and pagan revels. Jenny could always expect to be hit on by several Hollywood actors, and/ or actresses. She had considered, briefly, writing some salacious tales for the tabloids under a pseudonym, but just the recollection made her feel unclean, and she remembered the shower. Must conserve water.

. . .

The next day Dugan was approaching Mo's Barbecue when his cell phone rang. "Jack, I was about to call you. Just heard from Mark, says he was able to bring up something on the video and to come have a look. Meet me at Mo's, I'll buy you a pork sandwich."

"Ahh! Just had a bowl of clam chowder at the Splash Cafe. I'm down here at the pier, not catching fish. I need to check in with Stu at the bait shop, then I'll meet you at the hotel."

The Pismo Beach Hotel, decorated in the hacienda style, had a storied past. Visitors from elsewhere during the great depression must have thought the coastline from here to San Simeon had been imported from another planet. Limousines and grand touring cars were everywhere, movie stars, heads of state, gangsters, real estate developers… slumming on their way to or from big Dick Hearst's monumental palace on the hill north of Cambria. Not unusual to see Spencer Tracy, Bette Davis and W. C. Fields at the bar. Clark Gable and Joan Crawford held residence when shooting the film "Strange Cargo" in 1940.

Some four decades later, writer Hunter Thompson had a hooker in his room when things got loud. He was arrested for disturbing the peace, and having a thermos bottle full of reefer, and fined $130. "Yeah," he wrote later, "it was horrible. They beat me on the back of the legs. It was a case of mistaken identity."

Dugan found Jack in the lobby, reading a book. "Didn't expect you back in town so soon."

"Actually never left," Jack said, looking up. "Gloria and I stayed here last night, just for a change. She's shopping in San Luis. Lady at the desk said Mark would be here shortly." At which Mark rolled into the lobby on rollerblades and collapsed in an easy chair.

"Man," he wheezed. "Gotta get the exercise, but the traffic around here sucks."

"Why don't you go surfing?" Jack inquired.

"The ocean scares the shit out of me," he said. "C'mon back, I'll show you what we got." Mark's studio occupied a small side room that was likely once an office or store room. A half dozen large monitors covered the short wall, fronted by a control board and array of digital devices and cables. He punched a few buttons.

"Most of your footage was bad because of the backlight, except for a few frames, must have been a cloud, the light improves and I could magnify the image a bit. So have a look."

The largest monitor brought up a shimmering gray-green picture, showing the V formation at about double its former size. The five objects no longer resembled balloons, but bell-shaped creatures trailing long fibers, and between them a dark shape apparently cradled on a piece of fishing net.

Dugan and Jack craned toward the screen. "Are those what I think they are?"

"I hope so," Dugan said. "Unless you tell me we're not really looking at a squadron of jellyfish. Is that what you see?"

"We are agreed on that, my friend. But of more social and political import, the big question, the crux of the biscuit, is do we see the same thing in that net they're carrying." They both leaned in further. "Jesus Christo," said Jack. "You know what that is don't you?"

"I do, " Dugan replied. "That there is a Thompson submachine gun."

Thirteen

Most of the lunch crowd had departed Harry's. Dugan ordered a shot of Jameson and a glass of Stone Ruination IPA. Jack called for a shot of Patron tequila and a Blue Moon with lime in lieu of an orange slice. A few minutes were devoted to silent drinking. Thoughts were mulled.

Jack decided to come at it through the side door. "Last night Glo and I had dinner up the street at Giuseppe's. Always eat there when we're in town. We're thinking about Italy for retirement."

"You can get good Italian food in Boise."

"Yeah, but by that time Boise could be beachfront condos and a population of trust-funders and Lycra yuppies, and ex-cops. Anyway, we walked around town, looked in the old theater, which then became the bowling alley, and is now a huge pool hall with a decent bar. I mean, the place hasn't become a theme park like Avila, but the whole downtown is for tourists now. Harry's is all we have left…

"Anyway, this morning we walked up to Penny's Cafe for breakfast, and found that we'd both had strange dreams last night. Tell you about those later. But we were reminded that the few times we'd stayed here before, we had agreed that there is just some kind of weird juju in this town. Nothing specific, dig, just some off-center vibe that you can't identify. Like you're watching a movie where the characters might be a bit eccentric, but then things start getting really creepy. I think if a person stayed here too long he'd get creepy. Nothing personal."

"Point taken. But there's creepy and then there's downright surreal, like being followed by jellyfish with a machine gun."

"And that. And if that is, in fact, a true fact, I'm afraid the reality behind it is beyond even our considerable powers of comprehension. We may be in over our heads, pun intended."

"Agreed," said Dugan. "But you know what, after your elaborate preface to the subject, and a shot 'n a beer, it comes to me more clearly. The realization is this: That whatever it is, whether it's something within our regular space/time continuum or not, animal, human or rutabaga, it is but a message and not a threat. And that another message is forthcoming. Of course, the next time it may be a threat.'"

"You're beginning to sound like Sherlock Holmes."

"Precisely, Watson. And it will take our resolute and concerted effort to find the creator behind these bizarre events. Someone, or something, I fear, far more sinister than Moriarty himself…"

Dugan lost focus momentarily. "My dear wife, rest her soul, had a brother who worked in some part of the movie industry down there in the coastal desert, La-La land. She said he was always working on this or that script, dunno if he ever sold one. Anyway, he spent a week with us one summer. When he left he said 'Pismo Beach is like walking into the set of a Humphrey Bogart movie directed by Wes Anderson, with a script by John Steinbeck and Stephen King.'"

"Sounds like a good movie," Jack said. "Wonder if they need any extras for the angry Mexican-Indian crowd scene."

"I think we've already been cast, my friend."

. . .

Hank realized he hadn't yet told Jenny his own weird wave story. "The reminder came from a guy named Jack Padilla, who came by the shack the other day and mentioned the guy you asked about, Byrnes."

"What did he have to say?" she asked.

"Said that he and Byrnes were doing some research work for the Chumash Tribal Council, and wanted to know if there was any way that Pearl could arrange the use of one of the remote-control subs. Maybe she could make it part of her study."

"I told Hank to message him that I'd check with the university," Pearl said. "It doesn't sound like something they would do, because of the liability as well as the expense. I'd have to be there as operator, but who knows?"

"The Indians carry some heavy water," said Hank. The conversation hit a freeze frame. Hank simply meant that the Chumash possessed some political clout hereabouts. That, being Indians, they had paid their dues, been admitted to the club through the back door, that they had a hall pass. But below that, at a conscious level obscured in Hank by the second glass of Opolo zinfandel that Jenny was serving, lay the definition of heavy water, which both Pearl and Jenny had right there at the forefront of their more finely-tuned female cerebra. The freeze frame hit quick defrost.

"Heavy water," Pearl said. She and Jenny looked at each other as if it were a lucid moment, which it was. "What?" Hank asked. "Something about the Chumash?"

"No," replied Pearl. "Heavy water is a scientific term. It means water that contains a radioactive isotope of hydrogen called tritium. It's rare stuff in its natural form, created by a reaction to cosmic rays in the earth's atmosphere. But it can also be made in the lab."

"Which has what to do with the Chumash?" Hank inquired. "Nothing," Jenny said, "but it may have something to do with curious goings-on in the ocean. From what I've read, heavy water is used in nuclear power plants and can also be used to produce nuclear weapons."

"That's true," added Pearl. "Plutonium can be produced without all the technology required to enrich uranium."

"You saying that we've been surfing in radioactive water?" Hank asked.

"No, not that's dangerous for humans, far as we know," Pearl said. "But it might well be harmful for other species. When you get all this other stuff in the mix – rise in water temperature, chemical pollution, other sources of radiation – we may be cooking up some strange creatures out there."

"Actually," Hank said, "Heavy water is deuterium, not tritium, although I guess the latter could be called 'even heavier water,' but the production process is similar. The Diablo Canyon reactors aren't heavy-water reactors, nor are those at Fukushima. Argentina, Canada and India are the heaviest users of heavy-water reactors."

Pearl and Jenny regarded him with some amazement, both rendered temporarily speechless. "And speaking of radiation," he went on, "I heard an NPR report that said the radiation levels down in Los Alamos, New Mexico, at the first atom bomb test site, were still ten times above normal. After seventy years. It just makes you wonder what sort of mutations may have developed over the years, among all species. Including ours."

"Have you seen the evening news lately?" asked Pearl. "Or any current political debates?"

"Speaking of mutations," Spence said, "have you guys ever heard of an amphibian called the vampire frog?"

Jenny and Pearl looked at each other, both thinking they would just wait for the punch line. This sudden burst of lucidity had to come with a tag. He would need no encouragement.

"No, really. This marine biologist I met at the hotel said he was involved in a major study, some school in New England. Said that evidence showed the existence of a vampire frog, that can suck the blood of frogs and other critters, even bigger ones like gophers, squirrels, cats. Even small dogs, they just drop out of a tree right on their neck."

"Did he say where this study may have been published?" Jenny asked.

"Didn't ask him that, but he seemed to know his stuff. He did have a cute name for the nasty little buggers." Pearl had to ask, just to be polite. "What did he call them?"

"Croaksuckers. And he said the little bastards could produce a killer belch."

Fourteen

Spence didn't mention the twin agents interview to his co-workers or supervisor. He figured whoever needed to know about it already knew about it, and so long as his job was unaffected, he might as well keep it off the record. He was glad to be back in the lab, and diving in warmer waters.

A week after filing his report he was called in for a meeting with the Coastal Research director and the head of the department. The director was a woman in her forties who looked like she could bench press LeBron James, but was a serious and capable scientist. The chief of the Biochemistry Department was a man in his seventies, Stanton Penfield, who looked like he'd been recently embalmed. It was said his family once owned Coronado Island. The diploma on his office wall designated a PhD in Chemical Engineering from Stanford.

"So Spence," opened Margaret Getz, "it doesn't look like the Pismo trip produced much data."

"Yeah, as you can see in the report, I didn't really find anything out of the ordinary, at least in the ocean. The only items of note were those contours in the bottom along the pier. Did we get anything back on the sand samples?"

"We just did," she said, "and your photos were good. The samples were fairly normal for that area in terms of composition, although there were slightly higher than average traces of calcium carbonate in them. What did you make of those formations?"

"Well, they just looked like symmetrical divots, about three feet deep, but all uniform in size and spacing, and directly parallel to the pier. I thought maybe there had been some weird wave motion at work, perhaps something to do with their proximity to the pier. Puzzling, but a bit outside my expertise."

"So, you didn't see any kind of marine life that was unfamiliar or... anything in the water that seemed out of place?"

"No, not really. Did see some thresher sharks and a lot of jelly-fish."

"What did you see that was out of the ordinary onshore?"

"Beg pardon?"

"You said that you found nothing curious 'at least in the ocean.' Leaving the implication that some sort of onshore activity caught your attention."

Spence then realized that Margaret likely knew about, and had probably approved, the feds intervention, and wanted to hear his side if the story. That maybe she and Penfield were as much in the dark as everyone else, and just hoped to get more information. Who knew what the agents had told them, if anything?

So he decided to heed his grandpa's advice and "come clean, boy, 'cause lyin's only gonna make it worse." Spence summarized meeting Byrnes at the bar, the backwards boat story, surfer Hank and the rogue wave, Jenny the journalist, the panga boat, the federal suits and the surveillance video. After about four minutes his mouth and memory both ran dry.

Getz and Penfield looked at him in silence for several seconds. They took on the appearance of a couple who'd been watching an absorbing TV drama, the commercial break had arrived, and they were deciding whether to get up and go to the bathroom. They also shared the wan look of people who'd just realized they'd been spending too much time in the office.

So Spence broke the silence. "If I may ask, can anyone tell me just what I was looking for in Pismo? Is it, like, classified information or something? Because quite a few people seem to be involved."

"No and yes," replied Margaret. "No, we can't tell you and yes, it is classified information. And we don't know what the information is, and likewise why it's secret. We were given very little to go on, which is why your mission was so undefined. We think it was probably just a one-time assignment, and we now have another one for you, which is completely unrelated."

"But first," Penfield finally spoke, in measured terms. "First we would like to know if you saw any frogs."

Frogs? "Uh, no sir. My dives were all in the ocean, but I expect there are frogs in the estuaries. The only salt water frogs I've ever heard about are in Asia."

"Hmm," he replied. "Though we do seem to keep getting more imports from that part of the world."

With the observation hanging there like a tired tree frog, and no clarification apparently forthcoming, Spence asked what his new assignment would be and where.

"More diving," Getz said, "with more explicit objectives this time. In Japan." Before he could ask about the schedule, she said there was one more question. "Did you read the report we provided for background on the Pismo study?"

"Absolutely, real interesting stuff. Which is why I was surprised that my instructions didn't include any dives off Diablo Canyon."

"Well, that was part of the original framework, but the permission process got delayed, and that's when Washington got more involved. That should be resolved soon, and if so you should be going back, but this time you'd work out of Avila Beach. And have a dive boat, and hopefully more specific instructions.

"But regarding that report, did it give you any sense of what the government could be looking for? We wonder about this apparent urgency when the data is so vague and insubstantial. At least in what they've shown us."

"Well, just based on the report, and this is just speculation, it looks like someone in Washington has undertaken to prove or disprove the hypothesis that EMR can cause genetic disorders or modifications in some marine organisms. As to who or how or why they came up with the theory... I have no idea. But I expect what they're looking for is an animal of some kind that is something other than a random mutation, a creature that has short-circuited the evolutionary process. But I'm just guessing. Be nice to have more to go on."

She seemed to find his answer satisfactory. "Okay, Spence, I guess that's it for now. We can go over the Japan project tomorrow. Do you have anything further, Stanton?"

"No frogs, eh?"

Fifteen

Dugan shared Jack's lament about Pismo's slide into nearly total tourism, but reminded him that if it weren't for the flow of visitors they wouldn't have food choices like Mo's, Splash Cafe, Steamers, McLintock's... not to mention the old hotel and other charming roadside attractions.

"Not many beach towns can get by on just local commerce these days," he said, "not with the depletion of the fisheries. It's a matter of geographic determinism, because folks will always come to visit the shoreline. I think there may be some genetic impulse involved."

Jack sensed a speech in the making, and ordered two more beers. "Genetic?"

"Yeah, we humans seem to have some vague biological memory stashed away in our DNA, an unconscious but abiding sense of where we came from. And even though we're fully aware that we can't breathe underwater, without accessories, that need to connect with the ocean persists. Like maybe oxygen, while it keeps us alive, is just not enough somehow, serves the body but not the soul. But when you add a couple hydrogen atoms, a little salt for seasoning, dash of calcium for the bones, a pinch of potassium for passion... you got yourself a genuine baptismal bath of the gods."

"I know the chemical elements in salt water," Jack replied. "What I don't know is what to make of gun-toting jellyfish. Do you?"

"Sadly no. But now I'm thinking that was a patrol with a specific mission. And I'm speculating that those jellies were directed to deliver that Thompson to us, to provide confirmation of the first mate's story, and maybe even to establish a link with their headquarters, wherever and whatever that might be."

"A message that says..."

"Well, this may be a real stretch, but I get the feeling that this creature, whatever it is, is the commander-in-chief of the jellies, the underwater tugboat, and who knows what else, and is looking for allies on land, and that there's no sinister plot here after all. That these little skirmishes we've heard about are just a means to get attention, to connect with someone who isn't a threat. Maybe someone it can trust as a conduit to the outside world."

"You know, Byrnes, coming from you that sounds only half-crazed. Question is, why would it choose you?"

"Who knows? My magnetic personality, my reverence for all forms of life, my Sean Connery smile? My harmonica playing? But I do have to wonder why I was the only one who saw that boat going out to sea backwards. Seems kind of cosmic, don't you think?"

"Quite, but now what? And what about Mark? What if he starts talking about what he saw, or tips the authorities about the video? And remember the two feds Henry said were asking about you. You're already on somebody's list."

"That was curious," he admitted. Dugan had no idea how he might have become a person of interest, though he liked to think of himself as an interesting person. Since the agents hadn't come around to see him, the issue had to go into the non-problem column for the moment. "I don't think Mark will be a concern. I gave him a hundred, with the request that we stay off the record for the time being, and the implication that he might be primed for some poten-tially groundbreaking video work. Plus, who's going to believe a kid who says he saw five jellyfish transporting a machine gun?"

"Good point, but you never know what will freak people out, or what their response will be. The owner of that boat, and the Aussie you talked to, were both questioned by the feds, so they know about the Thompson too."

"True fact, Jack, but they probably don't know that we know. And to them it's still just an unsubstantiated story. Hell, I was dubious until I saw that video. In any case, maybe we should take a step back for awhile. First I have to get back to that reporter, Jenny, see if she knows any more by now. Then I may just take a ride up the coast, take a break from this weirdness. Let the brain cells regroup, give the synapses a nap."

"Mmm, wish I could come along. My old Moto Guzzi could use a road trip and so could I, but I gotta work. By the way, I did ask Hank Wilson about the Cal Poly drone subs and his girlfriend is checking with the university. Her message wasn't what you'd call encouraging, but it was nice to get a response."

"Cool deal. That could be a valuable resource, we could use some technology. I'll touch base with her before I go, should only be gone a few days."

"So you're not going up to Portland."

"No, that's too far on the old Duck, at least for my old butt. Probably just to Monterey, go pay my respects at Robinson Jeffers' place, hang out at Point Lobos for awhile. Maybe stop at Esalen, empty the mind completely."

"Mmm, hawks and wolves, man. That could bring along just the sort of spiritual insight we could use about now."

Outside the late afternoon sun was on schedule to sparkle the lunch time verandas in Hawaii, and flared off the front of the rearview mirror on an old Dodge pickup idling down Pomeroy Avenue toward the pier. Behind the wheel sat a golden brown surf bunny with blonde hair in a pigtail, who may have been seventeen or forty, her head bobbing slightly, fingers tapping the wheel.

As she passed the two geezers stood in front of Harry's, both shamelessly transfixed, and through the open windows the voice of Stephen Stills trailed along...

Off the wind on this heading lie the Marquesas,

We got eighty feet of the waterline, nicely making way,

In a noisy bar in Avalon I tried to call you,

But on a midnight watch I realized why twice you ran away...

Both men had a brief flashback, when they'd each seen the Southern Cross for the first time, and respective blonde girls in pickups. Jack's gaze had turned inland, looking up, and he gave Dugan a nudge. He followed the line of sight to see a large red-tail hawk, sailing on the offshore wind.

"That's a good sign," he said.

Sixteen

Pearl was pleased that she and Jenny had made a personal connection. She knew Jenny wasn't sure what to make of Hank, but that wasn't unusual among their new acquaintances. Some folks tended to think he was just acting dumb, but she wasn't always sure it was acting. Although Pearl was nearly a generation younger, the women had found a common link in terms of curiosity and the random risk of adventure, in addition to world peace and saving the planet.

They moved to clean up after dinner (grilled Ahi, sweet corn and garden salad with fresh tomatoes), while Hank set off on foot to tour the ranch. "This is quite a nice spread," Pearl said. "And you live out here alone?"

"Mostly," said Jenny. "Eighty acres is plenty enough for me. Ely was here for about two years, but decided if the summers were this hot he might as well be in the desert, and moved to Moab. We visit now and then. He trains horses part of the time and has a river rafting business on the side. His last name is Roland, so they call it Roland on the River."

"And you have the whole bunkhouse?"

"Yep, it is pretty spacious. When this was part of a big working ranch they had twenty cowboys in here. No garage, but my old truck doesn't need one, and there's a shed for the dirt bike. I keep the ranch house in order, but it's not much bigger than this and hardly gets used. Once in awhile we have a little hoedown in the big barn with some of the local musicians, you'll have to come up next time."

Pearl recalled the last barn show they'd attended down in Los Alamos, when the combination of mushrooms and moonshine sent Hank into a marathon round of buck dancing, which nearly took out the makeshift bar, several other dancers and the drummer.

"We'd love to," she said.

"So," Jenny asked, "you haven't met this Byrnes character yet?"

"No, I've been out of touch with most of the beach people for awhile. I'm either in the lab, on the water or fast asleep. But I intend to rejoin society when the degree work is done, which is only a few months away."

"Well, now that I've heard Hank's wave story, I sure would like to talk to Byrnes. I met the guy you mentioned from Scripps, Spence, but haven't heard any more from him. I'm sure Byrnes would like to talk to you about the subs, so maybe we could get him to sit down for lunch next week."

"Yeah, good idea. We could meet at the Fat Cats Cafe and I'll give you both a tour of the lab at the Poly pier. Hank mentioned meeting Spence as well, but I think they only talked once. And he hasn't met Byrnes either, far as I know."

At which the phone rang and Jenny picked up. "Well hello..., yes, and speak of the devil we were just speaking of..." She listened for a few seconds.

"Yes I do know her, in fact she's standing right next to me drying dishes...

"That sounds good, and Pearl would like to come along, and has offered us both a tour of the marine lab...

"Yes, I think Friday would work." Pearl nodded. "Okay, give me a call when you get back, and ride safe."

"Jeez, I wonder if he's telepathic," said Pearl.

"Just might be. Said he's going on a quick motorcycle trip and will be back next week. Seems to be a pretty active guy for his age." They heard Hank stomping his boots on the porch. "If there's anything out there to step in, he will," Pearl noted. "You might do me a favor though, Jenny."

"What's that?"

"Don't tell Hank you have a dirt bike."

• • •

Gina sat down at Harry's bar just as Henry came in to start his shift. Her eyes roamed the familiar walls – old farm implements, antique weapons, mounted deer and antelope heads, the big pig upper torso in the corner, with three-inch hooked fangs in its gaping lower jaw. Below it an engraved woodcut sign:

– WILD BOAR –

– Paso Robles, Cal. –

– 550 Lbs. –

– 30/30 Winchester –

Henry came over. "Hi kiddo. You're here early, what can I get you?"

"Hiya Henry. Yes, got the chores done early today and had to stop by the nursery. How about a glass of the Chamisal chardonnay." As he poured the wine she asked if Byrnes had been around.

"He was in here yesterday with his friend Jack. They've got some sort of seafaring investigation going on. Not sure what it's about, but it seems to have captured a good portion of their attention."

"I've heard about it, in fact I was there by happenstance when the whole thing started, and somehow I've become part of the story. I assume he told you about the boat going backwards."

"He did, and I guess he went down to Lompoc, based on your tip, and found the boat. But he didn't offer any details. I don't ask questions, especially when feds are snooping around. The less I know the better."

"Feds as in federal agents?"

"Yeah, couple of 'em were in here asking about him a few days ago. Struck me as just low-level types. Told 'em a few fairy tales."

"Wonder why they'd be interested in him. Maybe there's a lot more to this boat incident than we may think. I hope he doesn't get jammed up over it."

"Dugan can take care of himself, not to worry. You two seemed to hit it off."

Gina felt the warming flush of the wine. Her teenage years were distant memories, but suddenly she was a sophomore again. "We do seem to have a few things in common. He's an interesting guy, for an old fart." Henry smiled and offered another glass of wine and a basket of popcorn.

"No, thanks. I still have to unload some plants and check on the animals. See you next week."

As she gathered her stuff, the light through Harry's ever open doorway was blocked by two large men who were obviously not locals. The first wore a black leather car coat over a navy turtleneck, with a gold chain and cross around his neck. The other had on a vintage varsity jacket, black with orange sleeves, and a gray T-shirt with a lettered life preserver logo, *Paramus Yacht Club.* Their combined avoirdupois exceeded the original weight of the boar on the wall.

"Afternoon gents," Henry said when they sat next to Gina at the bar. "What'll it be?"

"Two Bud Lights," said leather man. Varsity smiled at Gina. "How you doin'?"

"Fine, thanks," she smiled back. "Henry, I gotta run. Say hi to our friend when you see him."

When he returned with the beers, the first man, apparently the alpha dog, said, "Hope we didn't scare the lady off."

"Nope, she was just on her way. You guys from the east coast?"

"How'd you guess?" asked varsity.

"Your T-shirt. Didn't know Paramus had a yacht club."

"It's private," leather replied. "Speaking of friends, we're looking for one of our fellow members. Came out here a couple weeks ago to go fishing, said he was gonna charter a boat. Figured he probably came in here. Name's Marty."

Seventeen

Old habits. The road had always been Dugan's refuge when things stopped making sense, and his search engine had come up with nothing less rational than a gelatinous underwater weapons carrier. An image that wouldn't submit to any conceptual framework to which he had access. His hard drive not only lacked sufficient memory, the software had yet to be developed. But even an obsolete operating system can still ride.

Beyond San Simeon, the cragged spines of the Santa Lucia mountains reach the sea and sky in concert. Gaining elevation the road's switchbacks contract, then open to sweeping runs above the shoreline, then crimp again to hold the asphalt fast to the chiseled mountain faces. When the roadway is clean, and the wind blows softly off the ocean, when the Winnebago tribe has trundled elsewhere for the season, the coast road through the Big Sur is motorcycle heaven on wheels.

Dugan pulled in at Gorda to have a snack and let mountain time reset his mental chronometer. With miles to go on a road demanding complete attention, the one-beer mandate was in effect, consistent with his theory that anyone who can't drink a beer and ride a motorcycle should be prohibited by law from doing either. The fish tacos were mediocre, compensated only by the Firestone Easy Jack IPA. Drink local, act bifocal.

As he was gearing up to leave, a couple rolled in on a Yamaha Tenere with full touring kit. The bike was immaculate, as were the man and woman in matching nylon riding suits and helmets. Fifty-ish, married, they seemed to materialize out of a full page ad in *Cycle World* magazine. They'd ridden from Guatemala to Calgary, and were on their way back, all smiles. Ain't life grand, he thought. Have a good ride home. Adios.

Following another forty miles of lazy apexes, through one sparkling, brilliant coastal vista after another, the loping note of the Ducati holding the rhythm of the road, content in the middle of its power range, he pulled up at Nepenthe Restaurant, last stop before mid-Sur. Residual beer drained, Dugan considered the panoramic stretch of coastline to the south. The original homestead here in 1924 was a Christian Science meeting place, sold in 1944 to Orson Welles as a gift to his wife Rita Hayworth, though they never moved in. A penniless freeloader named Henry Miller lived just down the road.

The literary geography of this jagged landscape had also included Robert Louis Stevenson, Jack London, John Steinbeck and Jack Kerouac. Now, in the early afternoon sun, Dugan traced some fifty miles of shoreline looking south, before the headlands at Cape San Martin faded into the mist. From this vantage, the third canyon down had been home to Kerouac's final surrender to alcohol and deranged infirmity. What the writer called "ecstasy of the mind."

The tale of Kerouac's decline always struck a melancholy chord. Dugan rarely shared the story of his chance meeting with the writer, many years ago in a Union Pacific boxcar outside Camarillo. His famous road novel was still a couple years away, and the account of their meeting would be published a year later in a book titled "The Dharma Bums," in which the writer cast Byrnes as an aging stumblebum riding the rails. Though he had just come from Korea, via Pittsburgh and many stops across the country, and had paid little attention to his appearance. Hard times. Two young men seeking meaning in a world eroding in fear and suspicion, in which an international bullshit exchange came to be called a cold war.

He recalled the writer's enthusiasm, overflowing with Buddhist aphorisms, on his way to meet poet Gary Snyder, and thence to the solitude of a remote ranger station in the Sierras to write the book. When it came out, Dugan found the narrative disappointing, but for the first chapter, where the author recounted sharing his wine and cheese with him on the train, and declaring that they were both Dharma Bums.

From Nepenthe the road rises inland, as ocean views recede and reappear, snaking through chaparral, oak, pine and redwoods, shadowed by 5,000-foot granite peaks. The coast road requires constant maintenance and repair, as the forces of wind, tide, erosion and tectonic shift work to loosen its purchase on the land. A survivor of many years of unsanctioned roadracing and close calls here, Dugan was mindful of its hazards. Never come to think you know this road by heart, he cautioned young riders. One day you'll find it's changed, and can hurt you.

He rolled in at The River Inn, took his regular hidden parking spot around back behind the maintenance shop, and walked to the nearby Maiden Publick House for a necessary beer. Closed. Shit. On to the Inn, no worries, finding to his wonder and delight that every Wednesday this month was 10-cent beer day. Limit of two, which matched his own, if he set up camp by the river for the night. He figured the first beer would likely bring that decision into focus. Someone rolled up the volume on a Dead tune...

> Escapin' through the lily fields, I came across an empty space
> It trembled and exploded, left a bus stop in its place
> The bus came by and I got on, that's when it all began
> There was cowboy Neal, at the wheel
> Of a bus to never-ever land

The Sur still resists civilization. Little more than half-way through the first beer, another elder took the next stool and said, "I'd bet you're an old hippie, right?"

Dugan thought oh my, what have we here? The guy had shoulder-length hair, a beat-up lumberjack cap with ear flaps, and overalls. Probably lived in a cave up the river and cadged tourists for change or reefer.

"Is this a contest?" Dugan asked.

"What do you mean?"

"I mean, like, is there only room for one old hippie in this place? I hope that's not what you're saying."

"No, man. Chill out. Just thought you had the look is all, and the gear tells me you're a motorcyclist."

"True, you a rider yourself?"

"Mos def, my friend. Got a few bikes in the shop out back."

"You the maintenance man here?"

"Part time," he said. "Now and again I spell Morgan, the regular guy, when he wants to get away. Gives me a place to keep the machines and do some woodwork."

"Mind if I park my bike behind your shop?"

"You got a Ducati Darmah?"

"I do."

"Looks like you already have."

"Buy you a beer?"

Eighteen

Spence found himself with another potential dilemma. While nothing further had come of the Pismo episode, the Japan assignment had taken on an aspect of serious concern. As Director Getz outlined the mission, an undesignated branch of the U.S. government had agreed to assist the Japanese authorities in having a look at the oceanic effects of the Fukushima nuclear disaster. Scripps, among other marine specialists around the world, had been enlisted to aid in this enterprise. The radiation dangers, she asserted, were minimal.

Her confidence sounded less than reassuring. He was to meet in Hawaii with a diver from New York for a briefing, and be joined in Tokyo by the Japanese member of the team for equipment instruction and training. The prospect of diving with strangers did nothing to raise his confidence factor. Spence found himself hoping the Diablo project would hit the front burner, and his spot on the Japan team would have to go to someone else.

Meanwhile he'd been pondering old Penfield's obsession with frogs. What the hell was that about? The only ocean-going amphibians he knew of were part-timers at best, a few swamp frogs and salamanders, and none on the Pacific coast. So what had provoked the old man's interest? Had to be more than just idle curiosity, though Stanton did likely have plenty of free time. No, there had to be a stimulus for a notion like that, unless the chief just had some bizarre theory on a new species of saltwater frogs. Or was just recalling his days as a Junior Frogman in the middle school at the naval base in Annapolis. Or what?

The other open question stumbling around in the shifting maze of his brain was more insistent and tangible, the recurring wonderment at what Pearl might be doing at a given moment. He had known a few lovely women, been intimate with several of them, and rarely denied them his precious bodily essence, and had even been engaged for two years, but had never experienced this sort of fixation. The harder he tried to stop thinking about her, the more he couldn't.

Not one to seek the counsel of friends on matters of the heart, he imagined that if asked they would likely urge him to give her a call. Which seemed a sensible decision. He made a mental note.

. . .

Pearl sat at her gray steel desk, collating the final pages of the clam study. The results weren't encouraging in terms of any significant regeneration of the species in the bay, but showed a few interesting developments that might indicate the need for further study. The population had changed little over five years, but the clams were on average larger than those in a similar study of twenty years ago. In some cases, much larger. A few were triple the previous maximum, with some samples more than a foot in diameter.

Causation unknown. Interesting. Chemical analyses of the samples, carbon dating, X-rays and so forth would figure in the follow-up research of another student. Nonetheless, she savored the end of the process, and once it was submitted at school she could devote more time to the subjects of echolocation and magneto-reception, in the study of how marine animals communicate, navigate, socialize… perhaps even how they think. And what.

Freediving could certainly figure in such a study, with the advances in equipment – wetsuits, fins, lights and cameras – offering more possibilities in time and distance underwater. She could quote the description of REMUS (*Remote Environmental Measuring UnitS*) that someone had written for the lab brochure: "a compact, lightweight, autonomous underwater vehicle designed for operation in coastal environments up to 100 meters in depth. A remote-controlled mini-sub, in other words, that can perform multiple tasks. And is not afraid to look a seahorse in the mouth."

Pearl started thinking about how to disguise REMUS, to look more like a fish (shark?) than a mechanical device that might appear threatening to creatures that could eat her alive. She could cut the motor at the point of neutral buoyancy and freefall, with electronic assists for GPS, video recording, transponder, sonar and nearly silent horsepower on demand. Cool. She been making notes for the proposal for months, citing existing studies and gathering images.

Now she wrote in the margin – *Scripps, possible grant? Call Spence.* The purists were likely to point out that descending into the ocean with an electronic device could hardly be called freediving, but to Pearl its descriptor mattered not. Whatever it may be called, she was heading for deep water. Unfortunately the photographer, someone's roommate, who took the shots to include in the proposal, decided to use some in his resume. A photo of her astride REMUS showed up online, provoking quite a few comments, some of them genuinely rude.

One writer objected to the Betty Boop eyes on her skullcap. Another asked if the monochromatic color scheme of diver and drone had a scientific basis. No matter, her recent projects using REMUS had revealed creatures she'd not seen before in their own neighborhoods, amazing colors, bioluminescence, and the few sharks had been observant but disinterested. And once there had been something, though it came and went in a flash, and she couldn't be sure, but it looked like a big frog.

Looking at the photos, Hank felt compelled to admit that in the shot made public, she did appear to be involved in an intimate relationship with a torpedo. Pearl decided to let it pass with only a look of mild scorn, and a mental footnote to not reveal that, when they were alone together, she did refer to REMUS as her good friend Rey. *Rey del Oceano.*

Henry said truthfully that he didn't recall meeting a Marty recently, and asked if the Jersey boys might have a photo, at which Vince (leather) produced a mug shot and handed it to him.

"He does look a bit familiar." Then he looked at Lou (varsity), back again at the photo, and then at Lou again. It was the same face.

"You guys aren't fuckin' with me, are ya?" Henry asked. "I mean, I know that I look like an Irish cop…"

"No, man, relax," said Lou. "That's Marty, my twin brother."

"Oh, jeeze, that's a relief, 'cause I was just about to say that's gotta be the ugliest motherfucker I've ever seen."

Their faces froze. The word disbelief would later come to Henry's mind in recounting the story. Shocked disbelief. And then he smiled. Henry had great teeth, most of them original equipment. His smile could melt the habit off a nun, and in fact once had. She still sent him a Christmas card every year. Vince was first to pick up on the joke.

"Aww, you wise-ass," Vince said. "He's just jokin'," he said to Lou, who still didn't look too sure. "No, seriously, Marty was supposed to be back a week ago, and we haven't heard nothin' from him. Gettin' a little worried."

Henry admitted that he didn't remember seeing anyone resembling Marty, or Lou, in the recent past. "But so many tourists come and go through here, he could have come in and sat at a table. If you wanna leave the photo, I can run it by the waitresses and you can check back later."

Vince found that agreeable, left a generous twenty on the bar and stood up to leave. But Henry couldn't leave it alone. "You know, now I remember why that name rings a bell. About a week ago there were two other guys in here asking about somebody named Marty, but they didn't have a picture. Just said he was a big fella in his fifties, dark hair."

"Do you know who these guys were?" Lou asked. "Yeah. They were federal agents."

Vince and Lou again regarded one another in mutual surprise, then looked at Henry to see if he was smiling. He wasn't.

Someone selected an old Bobby Darin song on the jukebox:

> *Somewhere beyond the sea*
> *Somewhere waiting for me*
> *My lover stands on golden sands*
> *And watches the ships that go sailin'*

Nineteen

Dugan had assumed the traditional posture in the river behind the restaurant. Sitting in a lawn chair, in the shallows with your feet in the water, had become the River Inn's signature symbol. The appeal of relaxing in but mostly out of the river was pleasing for the weary traveler, feet gently massaged by the current, tuned to the soft burble and warble of the water, holding a pint of Anchor Steam IPA. Just how God meant it to be.

The maintenance man, Simon Wright, turned out to be rather more than a part-time janitor. The small barn was divided into quarters; shop area, bedroom, kitchen and motorcycle store room. Dugan was expecting an old Harley, maybe a couple dirt bikes and assorted bits and pieces. But when the door opened, it was akin to the first time he saw a girl naked. Holy moly, would'ja look at that. Gosh.

Four motorcycles aligned both side walls. On the right a '74 Ducati 750 Supersport and Moto Guzzi V7 Sport, a Harley XR-1000, and a Cagiva 750 Elefant. Facing them sat a Bimota db2, Triumph Speed Triple, a cafe-Honda 919 and an early Yamaha Venture. Dugan was well and duly gobsmacked.

"The space in the middle is for the Aprilia Tuono," said Simon. "It's in town getting new tires and brakes." The guy was clearly a rider, and a look at the tires showed that he knew how. Dugan felt he might well be glad to call Simon his new best friend.

"So town for you is Carmel?" he asked.

"Yep, it's only 25 miles. My regular house is up there, but I spend most of my time here. I have a permanent room at the Inn, just sleep out here when Morgan's gone. Can't have the bikes spending the night alone."

"Retired?"

"More or less. I had a small company that I sold to a big company for a lot of money, and my wife felt that half of it would suit her purposes in another venue. She now has a fashionable antique shop in Marin County."

Dugan figured Simon was probably fifteen years his junior, but had obviously picked up a full pack of experiences on the way here, and a few bucks. Judging by the walls in the shop and kitchen, he was indeed another old hippie. Grateful Dead and Jefferson Airplane posters, Fillmore concert flyers, a large print of a grinning Timothy Leary, and a painting of Jerry Garcia as the Buddha. The scent of patchouli oil lingered in the leather couch in the dining area. A serious Sixties man cave.

"So you're headed for Point Lobos tomorrow?" Simon asked.

"Am. I need a good walk, and a look at some different water. Then I'll probably go by Robinson Jeffers' place, pay my respects and then head home." As the men talked, over sips of Hennessey cognac, the evening trailed into the dark silence of the surrounding trees. Dugan recalled it had been his wife, the amazing Grace, who had turned his reading habits from Mickey Spillane thrillers to the west coast writers, and that he was forever grateful. They agreed that Kerouac had been more a prolific diarist than novelist, though his original blend of free-form jazz narrative would live on. Simon noted that his father, who migrated from England after World War II, had occasion to socialize with both Steinbeck and Henry Miller, and found both engaging company.

"I'd like to ride in with you tomorrow," said Simon, "but I have to take the truck and pick up the Aprilia. You're welcome to bunk here, it's pretty late to set up camp. And if you run out of daylight tomorrow, you can stay over again and head for Pismo in the morning."

As ever, Dugan added a name to the long hospitality list of motorcyclists he'd met on the road. One might not want to make a habit of depending on the kindness of strangers, but it was only good manners to accept when it showed up unsolicited.

. . .

Gina replayed the message from her ex-husband twice. On the third listen, she could almost pick up a narrative thread between the cursing and louder barks, ...YOUR SON... yadda-yadda and if THAT SONOFABITCH shows up... followed by some incoherence, which gave her a jolt that he might be drinking again, after nine years without.

But when she reheated the decaf in the microwave and sat down, only two words from his tirade occupied the otherwise blank screen on her memory monitor. The words were Edward Snowden.

She called his number, got the machine and gently said, "Hello Rick," and then yelled "WHAT THE FUCK!?" and hung up. A few sips in, she spiked the coffee with a splash of Old Grand Dad and moved to the back yard to sit in the trees. She'd not heard from their son Leon in a week, not unusual, since he was active Air Force at Vandenberg and was kept busy. She would call him at the base when she finished her coffee. Two hours later she awoke still in the camp chair, blinking at a starlit sky.

Gina called Leon's house and got the machine, said please call me and phoned the base. "Hello, I'd like to speak with Sgt. Brennan please."

"What department, ma'am?"

"He's in Satellite Communications."

"Thank you, please hold." As the minutes rolled by the worries rose up. Then another voice came on. "This is Lieutenant Spicer, may I help you."

"Yes, I'm trying to reach Leon, this is his mother. Is he there?"

"I will check, ma'am, please hold." This time the wait was mercifully brief. "No, ma'am, he's not on the duty roster. His team leader said that Sergeant Brennan went on two-week leave yesterday."

Gina felt relief, he could be getting ready for a trip with his girl-friend, and would likely call her tomorrow. She always liked to start with the best case scenario. Meanwhile she would wait to hear back from Rick, and hope he wasn't on his way over. But either possibility seemed like a good reason to head down to Harry's.

· · ·

Henry was at his best on the slow weeknights. He could schmooze with customers, accept a complimentary drink himself now and again, and just enjoy the abiding comfort of a traditional laid-back beach bar. Good as it gets, unless he had to get physical with a rowdy biker or cowboy, since there was only one bouncer during the week, who was usually flexing his muscles and flirting with the college girls. But most of the time this was Henry's home and private reality show. The small arsenal under the bar had never been deployed, but for the leather sap required at times by those few miscreants who might otherwise insist on remaining conscious.

Neither the Jersey boys nor the federal suits had reappeared, but Henry always welcomed random entertainment at the bar and knew that in due time more players would arrive. All the world that's not a stage is a bar. He was reminded of the scene twenty- five years ago, well before his employment at Harry's, when he was just another patron and a young surfer on the loose. The club then had a more well-deserved reputation for the occasional knucklebuster, and every few months an undercover cop would bust them for selling to minors, but nothing real serious. Then one night a real brawl broke out, a racial beef between an anglo and an afro. Another white dude stepped in on the black guy's behalf and was stabbed, fatally. Henry had been there that night, but was out the side door, on his bike and half way home before he heard the first siren. No dog in that fight.

As a result, some of local merchants put the squeeze on the

police chief, who had little use for Harry's anyway, to put them out of business. Undercover cops set out to prove that drug dealing was involved, and the prevailing mood among the chamber of commerce, city council and fraternal business clubs was the notion that soon they would have downtown Pismo cleaned up once and for good. A few years later the drug charge was dismissed, the owner of Harry's had filed a ten million dollar lawsuit against the city, ran for and was elected major, won the suit and saw the police chief resign. The media coverage was extensive, often amusing, and at times read like a Perry Mason script.

Henry had campaigned on Harry's behalf, having watched the town's bar population shrink over time from sufficient to one. The day he had applied for the job, he wore board shorts, flip-flops and his "Keep Pismo Sleazy" T-shirt, which, with the Errol Flynn smile, put him behind the bar. Where he quite liked it.

Over the years he had learned to avoid personal relationships that extended beyond working hours. Moody women tended to reappear at the least opportune times, not to mention disgruntled spouses. He made exceptions of course, for people he liked and whom he knew could benefit from his experience and wise counsel. Byrnes was among the small group, and Gina, whose ex had solicited the sap on one occasion. And more recently young Mark next door, who seemed to carry equal reservoirs of creative talent and hypertension. Sometimes Henry felt like Dr. Phil.

Only Gladys, a old regular, was at the bar, so he kept the fan on and let her smoke cigarettes. He served her third gin and tonic as she watched the silent TV news, again the pasty visage of John McCain. Henry had wanted to make his moniker Mr. Bluster among the Shrubbies, but they said it had already been taken by Dick Cheney. He recalled the T-shirts in Haight-Ashbury in 1967: Dick Nixon before he Dicks Us. Already too late.

"That guy's a war hero like I'm a rocket surgeon," she said. "I knew some brave guys who went to Vietnam, but that war didn't make no heroes. It's just all pretend. We ain't been in a necessary war since '45. Still managed to kill a few million people though."

The news scene shifted to old footage of then President Bush in his flight jacket, trying to look determined. "Jeezus, would you look at that face," Gladys declared. "You know what it looks like?"

Henry admitted he did not.

"A cat's rectum."

Part Three

"The amphibian is the bridge between the terrestrial and the aquatic. I invite you to consider that it may also be a bridge between our water planet and the largely arid galaxy. A bridge between earth and the stars. A bridge, most importantly, between the mind of man and the cosmic overmind. And, of course, it's the biological bridge between the fishes, which identify with Jesus Christ, and the reptiles, which many identify with Satan."

Half Asleep In Frog Pajamas
– Tom Robbins

Twenty

Point Lobos, deep with history as a spiritual power place, was half fogbound at mid-morning. Dugan hadn't planned to stay long enough to sit and read, or listen and wait. But walking always opened the library of memory, and recalled a few visitors' impressions of this shoreline, the only section of the Sur to historically generate ghost stories. The perils of Pismo had withdrawn to a small cupboard in the back of his brain, but the jellyfish remained, at swim on the edge of conscious perception, throbbing.

The Salinan tribe had befriended the fog-ghosts here a few centuries ago, considered them lonely spirits, hoped to cheer them up, and held parties for them. Then the Spanish Catholic fathers were so aghast that they conducted an exorcism and drove the sad ghosts away. According to legend, the exorcist priest later went mad and leapt to his death from a cliff. Robert Louis Stevenson found Lobos the creative setting for "Treasure Island," and Ella Young held that the natural spirits that had fled Ireland settled here. The sacred cypress trees were said to be home to the spirits of ancient Lemurian priests.

While he recognized the power of myth, Dugan claimed no particular psychic abilities of his own. Recent events, however, had him considering the possibility that Carmel Bay had ultimately become too crowded with aged phantoms, old souls, specters and nebulous entities. There goes the neighborhood. Maybe the more restless among them had moved south to Pismo harbor, setting up house in new territory, warmer waters. And that they weren't just some bummed up fog-ghosts, but an angry bunch with an attitude.

Indian summer sunlight filtered by the marine layer touched the treetops, and highlighted the small whitecaps in the shallow bay. Dugan had heard the tales of malevolent forces visiting Lobos, bringing sudden dread to tourists. Steinbeck's friend Doc Ricketts had experienced the phenomenon, walking the beach with two friends when they were all seized by a nameless terror, and had to leave promptly. Others reported similar frights, struck by mortal fear, of what they knew not. But today the state nature preserve glistened calmly in the warming sun, not a threatening demon in sight. (Yes, he reminded himself, I know you can't always see 'em.)

Though Dugan was also aware that he stood at the southern terminus of the ocean section known as the Red Triangle, its hypotenuse reaching north to Bodega Bay and its point touching the Farallon Islands, 27 miles west of San Francisco. The name derived from its distinction as the small portion of the Pacific that hosted half of the world's great white shark attacks on humans. As Jack would say, that's almost fifty percent.

With binoculars, he scanned across the bay to Tor House and brought into focus the cobbled edifice of Hawk Tower. Jeffers' union of poetry and stone was approaching its centenary, and would likely stand for centuries more. Should the rising ocean eventually cover this coast, moving the shoreline inland to the vicinity of Fresno, the poet's stonework would remain intact on the sea floor. Perhaps to serve as a way station, a rest stop for the sharks on their way to nibble on surfers in the shadow of the Sierra Nevada mountains. Who knows?

Dugan noted the drift of his imagination, and the image of the morning tour group on the grounds at Tor House. He decided to forego a visit to the preserved residence this time, recalling his first viewing years ago, and the rankle that it was now girdled on three sides by suburban houses, cheek by jowl on narrow streets. Jeffers had been forced to sell his surrounding property to pay the bills in the Fifties. As Rimbaud had observed, "Poetry doesn't pay the *boulanger,* not to mention the *joueur de pipeau,*" or words to that effect.

Not long after finishing the tower, Jeffers, then in his thirties, wrote his own epitaph in a poem titled "Post Mortem," noting how these man-made constructs would dissolve in time

> *... Though one at the end of the age and far off from this place*
> *Should meet my presence in a poem,*
> *The ghost would not care but be here, long sunset shadow*
> *in the seams of the granite, and forgotten*
> *The flesh, a spirit for the stone.*

• • •

Jeffers would live another forty years, write prolifically, sour further on the follies of mankind with the advent of World War II, and be staggered by the death of his wife and soulmate, Una. Like many men of high mentality and creative force, he found comfort and solace in physical activity, mostly fishing and the fitment of stones.

The shoreline now lay fully bathed in sunshine, as they say, and the prospects for any enlightenment by spirits pagan or divine looked slim. But, determined to reap the full measure of the $10 park entry fee, Dugan continued his northerly amble along the surf. If there were any sprites or demons about, he was equally open to cheerful news or prophetic bulletins on the underwater activities of strange creatures. Any information you have, he addressed the ocean, is welcome. Not a rhetorical question. He waited a few minutes.

Absent any revelation, he paused to consider the ocean's span, the calm surface, color shifts and the gentle curve of the horizon. Comforting views. And turning to retrace his trail beheld a young woman emerging from the surf, wearing a full wetsuit best described as complimentary, holding a diving mask and snorkel. A GoPro camera was fitted between her breasts. On the beach she pulled off her cap to reveal an abundance of red hair, and as Dugan approached, regarded him with an striking pair of emerald eyes. A flash of green.

Right on, Neptune, he thought, just in time and much better. Though they were within hello distance, no words arrived in the vicinity of Dugan's lips, so he offered just his best replication of Henry's smile. "Hi," she smiled as he drew near. "Luvely diy, in'it?"

Scotland? "Even lovelier than it was a few minutes ago," he replied. "Doing some underwater photography?"

"Yes, I just got this camera. The kelp beds out there are just awesome. It's like swimming through a forest."

"Did you notice anything unusual in the water, in terms of odd fish or mammals?"

"No… just a lot of sea urchins and small fish, a few seals. Are you a diver?"

"I do a little scuba diving down around Pismo. This bay looks pretty calm by comparison, I reckon you have much better visibility."

"It's good when the sun is out, down to about forty feet. The scuba divers usually wear lights if they're going deeper." Her dialect was clearly northern Irish. "Are you a Carmelite?"

"I live in Monterey," she said. "I have surfed at Pismo Beach a few times, it's pretty cool. The water there is warmer this time of year, but I have to say the water here is cleaner."

"Is that your Miata in the parking lot?"

"'Tis, and I expect that's your motorcycle next to it. It's lovely. A friend of mine in Big Sur has some Ducatis."

"Would his name be Simon?" he asked, thinking why that dirty old hippie, enviously. "It is! Do you know him?"

"We just met yesterday, actually. He put me up last night. I was just about to head home, thought I'd stop and buy him lunch if he's around. How do you know him?"

"He and my dad were in business together a few years ago, jeez, come to think of it, more like twenty years now. That's when I was in college and only came home a couple times a year."

"What business were they in?"

"You know, I was never really sure. They said it had to do with computer software and applications and such. They were never really specific, and I always had the sense they weren't telling me the whole story. I know they did make a lot of money."

"What did you think they were selling?"

"I think they were drug dealers."

The walk to their vehicles revealed that her name was Erin, born in Donegal, mostly raised and schooled in Dublin, and transplanted to California in time for the Y2K kerfuffle, as a computer systems analyst. "I'm an IT nerd," she said.

Of course you are, he thought, noting the absence of any nearby enclosure for the removal of her wetsuit, which seemed no bother as she wiggled it off in three graceful moves, revealing a pink string bikini and leaving Dugan with a pleasant visual memory for his old age.

"Really nice meeting you," she said. "Give my best to Simon, and tell him not to be such a stranger." She retrieved her car key from atop the rear tire and unlocked the door, which upon opening turned on the radio and the voice of Van Morrison. "That's weird," she said.

> We were born before the wind
> Also younger than the sun
> Ere the bonnie boat was won as we sailed into the mystic
> Hark now hear the sailors cry
> Smell the sea and feel the sky
> Let your soul and spirit fly into the mystic...

...

As she drove away, Dugan turned for a parting look at the peaceful bay and gentle cypress trees. The sacred seeds, as the story goes, had come from the Monastery Garden at Lhasa in Tibet, and were planted by Buddhist monks in the ninth century. In 1915 a visiting Tibetan lama confirmed that monastery records documented their journey, and that the trees grew only at Lhasa and Carmel. Thank you Buddha, thank you Lord. We accept Erin as a sign of spiritual goodness and mercy. Mercy, mercy...

Twenty-One

Spence sat at a shaded picnic table on his deck, overlooking Coronado Bay if you squint. His laptop displayed a page of scientific data on the range of sea life on the central coast, with accompanying charts on their chemical compositions. His own metabolism was currently absorbing the combined elements of taco chips, guacamole and an Eagle Rock pilsner.

As a chemical engineer he was aware of calcium carbonate's prevalence throughout the natural world, but not the breadth of its applications. The stuff is in everything from building materials, to sugar refinement, diapers, paint, adhesives and Tums. "It is commonly used medicinally as a calcium supplement or as an antacid, but excessive consumption can be hazardous." Right there in Wikipedia, gotta be true.

So the question Spence was beginning to pose, though not beg, was what effect could an oversized appetite for calcium carbonate have on life in the ocean? And on which plants or animals, and what might they have to do to relieve their indigestion? The sea is full of carbonates from coral and algae, plankton, starfish, sea urchins and mollusks. What among them could be involved in creating large sand bowls? And why? Intriguing questions, and he made a note to see if any colleagues at the Institution had more data, since it could likely figure in their studies on ocean acidification.

Sobered by all this academic speculation, Spence's slow but deliberate thought process then re-opened the Pismo file. Byrnes just seemed to be an anomaly in the situation, although there must have been a reason he had attracted the federales. Absent anything new on his next assignment, he thought it might be a good idea to drive up the coast for the weekend, look in at Harry's and just hang out for awhile. The Clam Festival was coming up, he would call Jenny, mayhaps hook up with Hank and Pearl, preferably the latter.

And there, as if by golly, at the end of the beer and the thought, the phone rang. "Hello, is this Spence?"

"Yes it is, who's calling?"

"This is Pearl, in Avila Beach." Spence made a quick note to do a little research into telepathy. He may possess powers of which he had been wholly unaware.

"Well hello, and I bet you've heard this before, but I was just thinking about you."

"A few times, but it's always nice to hear. So how are you?"

At which he embarked on what he would later realize was a far more detailed and lengthy response than necessary. Pearl subsequently filled him in on her dinner with Jenny and the imminent prospect of finishing her master's and moving on to something else. Namely freediving and habitat studies of large ocean fish and mammals, and the thought that perhaps Scripps might be interested. Perhaps in a joint effort with Cal Poly.

"Well, I can certainly find out who you should contact, and offer a first-rate reference. You obviously have the credentials. And I would also invite you to come down and dive in some nice warm, moderately clear water."

She laughed. Lovely laugh. He could picture her, laughing. "I'll keep that in mind," she said. "So when are you coming back up to Pismo?"

"If my assignment situation is still on hold, probably next weekend for the Clam Festival."

"Cool. Let us know so we can get together. And hey, if you get here Friday you can join us for a tour of the marine lab."

"Who's us?"

"Jenny and I are meeting Mr. Byrnes for lunch. We'll save you a seat."

Spence said he'd see if he could get Friday off, and if so would join them. The thought of investigating Byrnes the investigator added another flavor to what could be a delicious recipe for fun. Seasoned by the possibility that Hank could be busy at work.

. . .

The road sign never failed to bring Dugan a smile when he found himself southbound on Highway One out of Carmel.

HILLS
CURVES
NEXT 63 MILES

He should be at the Inn by noon, when the pub would surely be open, and therein decide whether to carry on home or accept Simon's offer of another night's lodging. The onshore gusts at the aptly named Hurricane Point buffeted bike and rider slightly, but thereafter the Cabrillo Highway embraced the motive body language of man and machine.

Even after all these years, Dugan took delight in the axiom of Newtonian physics that a body in motion tended to stay in motion. And more importantly, its Byrnes Corollary, that a man in motion on a motorcycle tended to be happy as a clam on wheels. That visual always put him in mind of his favorite sports car fifty years ago, a white Porsche Speedster. She had the molluskan profile, damn near aerodynamically perfect, and insufficient power to get into serious trouble. Portia was of course her name, who would have loved this road, he knew. Now, as pilot of the equally lovely Grazia, he meant to employ and fully enjoy her qualities, and treat both road and machine with the respect and attention they deserved. And to also indulge the seductress of speed at times.

Yankee Point Rock passed on the right, last of the mystical cypress trees, then a long expanse of beaches, coves and headlands stretching south. At full song, 4500 to 6500 rpm, the Ducati V-twin produced a syncopated baritone resonance, fading in the wind, echoing up the canyons and back. As exhaust notes go, and dramatic vistas, better motoring, in his own opinion and experience, existed nowhere else in the known world.

The sun had just passed the shoreline when Dugan rolled into the wooded area surrounding what passed for downtown Big Sur. At mid-week in the fall, fewer cars and campers were in evidence, and he parked again behind the maintenance barn. The pub was open, through the window he could see a barmaid who looked like 1965 in a tie-dyed tank top, though she was at least a couple decades too young, and a man at the bar. Walking in he realized it was Simon Wright, talking with the young lady. They both wore the expression of people who just learned their dog had been killed.

"Hey," he said. "What's going on?"

Simon turned to him. "News just came on the radio. Robin Williams killed himself." In the following seconds of silence, unable to produce any satisfactory response, Dugan said, "When?"

"Yesterday," the barmaid said. "Hung himself in his apartment."

"Man," said Simon. "He was about my age. What a brilliant cat, and a real sweetheart as well. He stopped here a few times when he was on the road. What a goddamn shame. Krista, what's that quote of his running on the social media?"

"You're only given one little spark of madness. You mustn't lose it."

They raised a toast to Robin Williams, in agreement that a bright light of comic, and cosmic, energy had been smothered. Self-extinguished. Jesus. They shared the sadness, passed it around, and pledged themselves, one to another, to do their best to hang on to their own sparks. Crossed their hearts, but didn't hope to die.

After the bad news and two beers, Dugan noted his fading interest in a late afternoon ride home. "I think I'll take you up on the offer of another night in the shed. And whenever we get off these stools, dinner's on me."

"That sounds quite satisfactory. Tomorrow I have to scrub in the tires on the Aprilia and I have a meeting down at Esalen. We can ride that far together."

"Cool deal. I had meant to stop there on the way back, but noticed coming up that the sign now says By Appointment Only."

"Yeah, they did that a few years ago, too many tourists. But I have a permanent pass if you want to join me. In fact, you may enjoy talking to Gus, who works there. He's designed a two-place submersible that's in prototype, says it should be good to 350 feet."

Dugan then realized that some force of providence must be at work on this trip. In their first conversation, he and Simon had covered some ground on music, literature and the Sixties, but the ocean hadn't come up. He could see they wouldn't run out of material at dinner.

Over a bottle of Boulder Ridge syrah and fresh calamari, the two elders of their tribe held meet on the current nature of reality in progress, sailing vessels, and the elusiveness of the physical/spiritual balance we all seek. Which they say is like love and marriage, can't have one without the other. Or can we?

Awaiting the miso-glazed grilled salmon with wasabi mashed potatoes, and pasta Castroville, with chicken and artichoke hearts in pesto sauce, the conversation turned to more immediate topics. Dugan was keen to know more about Simon's history with the ocean.

"I did a few years in the Coast Guard, mostly between here and San Francisco. So I'm pretty familiar with this section, including Point Lobos."

"Were you ever struck with The Terror, as they call it?

"Not in the sense of nameless dread, but I was fearful once, when our ship seemed to be under the control of an unknown force.

The Spanish called it Punta de los Lobos, after the sea lions, which they called sea wolves. But we came to think there were far more threatening creatures out there than lions or wolves. The cutter got spun around like it was a top, guy on the bow was pitched off. Then the ship was lifted clear of the water and transported about a quarter-mile into the bay. No wake. That was it."

"Did you lose a man?"

"No, he just swam ashore. And we never came up with a rational explanation for the incident, didn't even report it. Didn't want to have to explain it to the CO, go through a lot of investigation crap. But it was seriously spooky. Did you get the frights up there yesterday?"

"No, far from it. The vibe was entirely pleasant, in fact, and I met a lovely lady who asked me to say hello. Her name is Erin."

"Really? Haven't seen her in awhile. Her dad and I worked together many years ago."

"That the company you sold?"

"No, we had a short-term partnership in the import-export-import business. Meaning we would import large quantities of weed, drive around the country with vans full of bulging duffel bags and export it. And import a lot of money. Forty years ago there were lots of places around the country where you couldn't get good reefer. Conor had been in the music business, and I was doing freelance photography at the time, so we had plenty of contacts. I guess you'd say we were early distributors in the new green economy.

"Nowadays, my ocean connection is the submersible I mentioned. My friend Gus is a real underwater junkie and backyard engineer, designed and built a sub he calls Clamentine. I'd say it's about 12 feet, makes maybe 8 knots, has four cameras for 360-degree video, sonar, satellite phone, and an audio system that broadcasts the sounds of whales, dolphins and sharks. And records whatever comes back. The cabin is self-enclosed within the shell, so if there's a power failure it can be released and float to the surface."

"Are you helping with the build?"

"Sort of. Gus is the machinist and fabricator, I did the camera set-up, with a transmitter so it can be monitored on the surface, and the audio system. It's a challenge when you change the medium from air to water. Especially the video, with the varied light and clarity, but the audio is great because sound travels five times faster in the water."

Dugan now had to wonder if Simon and Erin were actual human entities, spirit guides sent by the native American ghosts, or just phantasms of his imagination. Perhaps the whole tableau, from the old hippie at the bar, to Point Lobos and the beautiful woman rising from the sea, Van Morrison, and back to a different bar and the same hippie, was merely imaginary. Maybe he'd gone so far into the mystic that he was simply projecting his own internal movie, talking out loud to characters he only thought were there. Yet no one had called the men in white jackets.

So Dugan had no reason to not tell Simon about the backwards boat, the kid from Scripps, the Feds' radiation study, Jack's story of the diver, the journalist, Gina and finding the boat, the video and the Thompson-toting jellyfish.

Twenty-Two

Gina parked her truck across the street from Harry's, shut off the engine and tried to strangle the steering wheel. All the energy she had was taken up in trying not to scream, then she gave up and screamed. Leon had told her little about cryptography and his job monitoring all manner of information sent by satellite around the world. Classified, Mom, I can't talk about it.

But to be in the military service, with access to the inner sanctum of confidential data, and have your name pop up on the same list as Edward Snowden… that could well be serious shit. So, given the probability that the situation would likely get worse, whether or not Rick had done something remarkably stupid, which wasn't unlikely, Gina felt the proper thing to do was talk to Henry and have a drink.

"Hello, sweet cakes," he said. "Truth be told, you do look like you need a drink."

After hearing the story, Henry went to full sincerity mode and said, "I think you're getting too far ahead of the action, babe. You never know what sort of crap Rick will come up with, and you haven't heard anything from the military. I think you just need to cool your jets and wait to hear from Leon." Gina's face softened, and Henry welcomed the call from another customer so he could hide his own face, should it reveal the mask of a bullshitter.

Sometimes you get more information than might be necessary on this job, but all's fair. Gotta take the tragic with the comic. But he cringed at the brief notion that any sort of talk about whistle blowers could put one on some "person of interest" list. That kind of paranoia hadn't shown up for years.

And who should walk in but Herb Tuttle, another longterm regular, who was the source of some humor just for his silence. A person wouldn't use up all his fingers counting the words Herb had spoken in the past ten years. College kids would try getting him to speak, but Herb just smiled, sometimes a nod. Or, if he wasn't in the mood, gave them the finger. Always drank the best scotch, neat. "Hi Herb, good to see you." Smile, nod.

Henry took Gina a drink on the house and a basket of popcorn for comfort. "You know," she said, "I ran into Herb at the hardware store awhile back and he talked my ear off. He was in the secret service in Number Two, went all over Europe and Africa, even spent some time in China. This is the only place where he doesn't talk."

"We all need our quiet time," Henry said. "Maybe he's formulating the next chapter in his memoirs. Sounds like it would be a good read."

. . .

Hank had only been waiting in front of the Cool Cat for a few minutes when his phone rang. Pearl. "Hey, I'm going to be a little late," she said. "Just have to log some data from Rey and I'm on the way. Say twenty minutes."

"Who's Ray?"

"Oh . . . , that's what we call the drone sub."

"Okay, think I'll grab a beer at Harry's. Meet you there."

He checked the bar for familiar faces, found none, but then spotted Henry talking to a woman near the back. "Hey, Hank. Long time no surf. Still got that old longboard?"

"Sure do. How've you been?"

"Still rockin' in the seal world. Yourself?"

"Hangin.' S'posed to meet Pearl for dinner, but she's running late."

"Gina, this is Hank, another old pal from the beach. A young old pal."

"Hello. I have a son about your age."

"Cool, does he live around here?

"Lompoc, last I heard. But now I'm not sure."

Now well into her second Greyhound, Gina took Hank's quizzical expression as a cue to relate her brief story to a complete stranger, who seemed like a nice boy after all. At the end he looked more concerned than alarmed.

"Jeez," he said. "That's kind'a hard to put together. I reckon he'll be in touch with you to fill in the blanks."

Whereupon, as that old fickle-fingered fellow would have it, Henry reappeared with an envelope with her name on it. "Verna was working last night when a young man gave her this. He asked her to make sure I got it, which she just remembered to do. I expect it's from Leon." Gina stared at the envelope, which was taped shut. She recognized his printing, the block style of draftsmen and architects.

"Are you going to open it?" asked Hank. "You wanna be left alone?" Henry said. "Not a problem."

"No, it's fine. Probably just his vacation itinerary. He and his girlfriend usually go down to Baja this time of year, but you'd think he'd leave me a message on the machine." Henry handed her a butter knife.

• • •

Jack backed his truck up to Dugan's carport, unlocked the chain and hooked up the boat trailer to his hitch. He checked the house for irregularities, though it had been empty only two days. Dugan had to be reminded to pay more attention to his own security. Jack had often chided him about the puny arsenal he kept on hand, consisting of his brother's Navy Colt .45 automatic and an M1 carbine that Henry had given him, since he had a spare. "Best light rifle ever made," he said. "If you can't fight your way out with this and a .45, you might as well be dead anyway." Jack had always enjoyed Henry's lighthearted touch.

Nothing was out of order on the property, and since his wife had a meeting after school, he headed for Harry's before going home. The public radio station was playing a Neil Young song

> Somewhere on a desert highway
> She rides a Harley-Davidson
> Her long blonde hair flyin' in the wind
> She's been runnin' half her life
> The chrome and steel she rides
> Collidin' with the very air she breathes
> The air she breathes.

Gotta service the Guzzi, he thought. He parked in the public lot by the pier for ease of egress and headed up the street. At mid-week nearing sundown the absence of heavy pedestrian traffic was refreshing, and Jack remembered that on his last visit to town, he had noticed that quite a few of the pedestrians were heavy indeed. A lot of those folks from the valley may not have necessarily been eating well, but certainly often.

The old Pierside Seafood restaurant was about to reopen as Wooly's beach bar, Pancho's surf shop and the Splash Cafe were busy as usual, and Jack paused to wonder if Brad's still had the best tri-tip sandwiches in town. He passed Mo's, inhaling deeply the aroma of barbecued pork, and crossed Pomeroy into the pool hall. The bar was nearly empty and only two tables in use, one with two young men in suits, and the other a couple burly guys who looked like New Jersey.

Out the door, he scanned the dozens of T-shirts displayed in the old movie poster cases. The vintage Zig-Zag rolling paper logo was still popular, "I May be Old But I Got to See All the Cool Bands," and "Not Tonight Ladies (I'm just here to get drunk)." And for real class, "I Wish my Job was a Bitch, and My Girlfriend Sucked."

Jack had a peek through the window at the lobby of the hotel, empty as usual, and took the next left through the front door at Harry's. Henry looked up as he approached the bar. A woman seated in front of him, her back to the door, was reading a note; to her left sat Hank the surfer, and on the other side was the lovely Pearl. Just as Henry raised his hand in greeting, the woman suddenly jerked upright as if she'd been slapped, and fell backwards in slow motion. Jack leapt the last three steps and scooped up Gina when she was just past horizontal, out cold, but in time to keep her head from hitting the floor. A sound he'd heard too many times. He carried her around the bar and laid her down gently on a pool table. Henry was already there with a cold wash cloth. The note was lying on the bar in front of Hank, so he picked it up.

DEAR MOM,
FOR REASONS YOU'LL LEARN SHORTLY, WE CAN'T CORRESPOND BY PHONE OR EMAIL. SOMETHING HAS COME UP AND I HAVE TO LEAVE. DON'T TRY TO CONTACT ME, I'LL LET YOU KNOW WHERE I AM. THERE'S A BAG ON THE SEAT OF THE TRACTOR, IT CONTAINS ALL THE INFORMATION. SOME DOCUMENTS (YOU'LL KNOW WHICH ONES) MUST BE INCINERATED AFTER READING. SAME FOR THIS NOTE. DON'T WORRY I'M FINE.
TELL DAD I'M SORRY
LOVE, LEON

P.S. JUST TO STAY SAFE, IF ANYONE ASKS, YOU HAVEN'T HEARD FROM ME.

Twenty-Three

Just before dawn Dugan awoke to river sounds, including a few frogs with sleep apnea. He knew how to locate and prepare coffee, but preferred to remain abed and consider the menu of options at hand. While the comfort of being out of cellphone range was pleasant, he was more or less obligated to re-enter the information network of people, agencies, hidden motives and, apparently, unknown creatures of the deep. The great ride, new friends and almost dreamless sleep in the forest would have to suffice. Could do worse.

He dozed again, descending into a deep water dream with an exquisite aquatic display of nudes on horseback. Athletic young women and men, riding glistening Arabian mares and stallions, swimming effortlessly in bright clear water. The women's hair flowed behind them, in concert with the horses' tails, as they soared and dove as if free of gravity, and appearing to have a wonderful time. At which point he smelled the coffee and woke up.

Simon was at the stove. "Morning. Got a skillet breakfast going if you're hungry, coffee's there on the counter." The early odors of fried onions, mushrooms, potatoes, and eggs brought him to one coffee shy of full consciousness. "Surely do appreciate the hospitality," he said. "And you're more than welcome at my place if you get down south."

"Cool. I do get as far as Ojai now and again to see my daughter, and an old riding buddy lives in Cambria. Maybe we can take a ride between there and Paso Robles." The talk drifted from favorite roads and off-road exploits, to life in the Sur and its abiding lure for travelers. "Yeah, it's hard to find this kind of terrain in proximity to the population centers anymore," said Simon. "Having the ocean on one side and mountains on the other prohibits the kinds of development that would ruin it, so I was just lucky to land here. Suits me perfectly.

I get the impression you signed off the grid some time ago."

"Nineteen sixty-eight," said Dugan. "The business and political frameworks anyhow. Never did head for the wilderness, I need to be near a large body of water. Electricity is also handy. Did have several straight jobs, good ones in fact, but since Grace died I've learned to live well on limited means. My footprint is small."

"Gus has a similar situation, he looks after the supplies and systems at Esalen, and has a nice shop. Remember the old James Bond movie with the submersible car? Forget which actor it was."

"Think that was Roger Moore, with Barbara Bach. Who married Ringo Starr."

"Yeah, go figure. I believe the car was a Lotus Esprit, not sure. Anyway, that's what Gus has built, an underwater car."

• • •

After breakfast, Simon rolled the Aprilia out and put on a vintage Belstaff jacket. "I just got an email from Erin. She had a photo she wanted you to see, and I told her we're just leaving. She's sending it on to Gus."

The road south still held some damp, shadowed turns at mid-morning, so the two riders kept a moderate pace and enjoyed the setting, the counterpoint pulses of their pipes muffled by the bordering trees. The highway rose with the mountains' changing pitch, then down to the lower bluffs and coves, past Nepenthe and the Henry Miller Library. Simon pulled in at Deetjen's Inn to check his tire pressures.

"All good," he said. "I'll signal at the turnoff, it's about a quarter-mile this side of the main entrance." Simon led out, and picked up the pace to about eight-tenths, giving Dugan a nice demonstration of how far motorcycle performance had come in thirty years. Ten miles down the sweeping road, Simon pulled in at what looked like a wide cow trail that descended to the campground, where Gus's shop sat alone above a rocky cove.

He was moving about in the kitchen and talking on the phone as they entered. "A what? ... No, Irv. Not a chance. There's no such thing, Irv. There's reality and there's a show, it's an either/or deal. You could have a show about reality, which would be pretty fucking boring, but not a reality show. Never the twain, dig? It's an oxymoron... What? ... No, I'm not calling you a moron... Listen, I got company, gotta go. Later."

"Gus, this is Dugan, another old hippie on the road. I was telling him about Clamentine."

"That's what Irv Khan was calling about. Wants to do a TV show about renegade scuba divers or some crap, black market abalone, foreign gangs... Asked if I'd want to rent her out as a camera vehicle. Hollywood nonsense."

Gus looked more like a roadie from an acid-rock band than a mechanical engineer, but he was quite interested in Dugan's capsule version of the Pismo capers. Especially Pearl of the Poly Pier, and her underwater drone.

"The REMUS is cool," he said. "I've got the ship rigged to carry two of them, so you can save their batteries until launch, then control and track them, and retrieve 'em. So there's no need for a support boat on the surface." Gus's experience with the federal bureaucracy had involved marine research at Monterey Bay, but grew troublesome, he said. Too many committees. Then he unexpectedly offered, given Simon's endorsement, to take Dugan on an exploratory dive in Clamantine off Pismo. "Hell, that's just a short run for us. And it needs more shakedown before it goes to a trade show. Just lemme know a few days in advance. It'll fit in Simon's truck."

This just keeps getting better, Dugan thought. "That is very kind. I'm going to see Pearl at the lab tomorrow, and I'll see what we can set up. Meanwhile, can I have a look at your sub?"

"Sure, it's right below us in the shop." Gus walked to a fire pole in the corner and slid down through a hole in the floor. "No room for stairs in here," said Simon, and did likewise. The shop was half again the size of the living quarters, with a double garage door opening on the beach. A blue tarp covered a dome-shaped object in the middle of the room. Gus pulled off the cover.

Another gobsmacker. There, in hand-formed aluminum, sat the perfect replication of a 1957 Porsche Speedster, sans wheels, with a clear plastic egg in the cockpit, four bullet taillights and a California license plate reading CLMNTYN.

"Friend of mine was restoring a Porsche and let me make a form, and I just filled in the wheel wells to make it seamless. The electric motor and drive pump are in back, and Simon's electronics are in front. I made aluminum copies of the Speedster's bucket seats. It's been a fun project."

Dugan now came to realize that he might possibly be on a mission from one god or another, or maybe a cosmic consortium. And that the illumination had come to him here, in the Sur's designated place of healing and peace. Fifty years had faded down the road since he'd last spent time here, and the image drew into focus – full moonlight throwing sparks on the ocean, the luminous presence of Joan Baez, and the dawn of era soon to end. The masters of war were having their own gatherings on the other coast, and within five years all was changed.

Nonetheless, although the door had closed by the time Nixon came along, Dugan and countless others had already gone through it. Now he was all but suffused with contentment, well pleased with this fine company of fellow refugees and co-conspirators. And he had been transported by motorcycle, that most spiritual conveyance. Blessed beyond all reason.

"Hey, before you go," Gus said, "there's an email message for you from Erin, with a photo." The trio ascended the outdoor stairs, and Gus opened a laptop computer on the kitchen table. The message read:

Hi, I was going through my shots in the bay, and remembered your question about seeing anything strange in the water. Well, I only saw this later on in a photo of the bottom. The object at lower left is a sea-urchin, maybe four inches in diameter. The large shape on the right has just moved off the floor, they're almost in the same plane, so the size differential is one to one. You tell me what it is.

Erin

The men bent to the screen to make out the creature on the right, which was apparently in the process of leaving quickly, perhaps in fear of something closing in from off-screen, or in pursuit of lunch. Or from camera shyness. "Well," Simon said, "it looks like a frog."

"Quite a large one, if so," said Gus. He held a set of digital calipers over the sea-urchin, then opened them to measure the mottled green/black form next to it. The instrument wouldn't span the object's length. "Much larger than your average amphibian. On his hind legs, that critter would stand just a bit over eight feet."

"Never heard of giant frogs in the ocean," Simon observed.

"Or jellyfish SWAT teams," said Dugan.

Twenty-Four

Pearl scanned the lab's aquarium tanks, the diving gear hanging on the wall, REMUS I and II snuggled in their cases, and realized she'd soon be missing this place. It had been her home, virtual and literal, for nearly two years, and become comfortably familiar. Nonetheless, this phase of her formal education was complete, time to move on. And, she reckoned, should a grant come through, the site might still be her work station for independent research. Perhaps even as a faculty member. Job security and an ocean... Dare to dream.

The subject would need discussion with Hank, who had talked of selling his surf shack at the hotel and spending some time surfing in Australia and New Zealand. Which she would definitely dig for the freediving it would afford, but talks would have to wait in any case, since Jenny was due to arrive tomorrow. And Byrnes, and maybe Spence. Could be an engaging day with the fellow humans.

The business with Gina at Harry's was troublesome, but she seemed to have a helpful group of friends on hand. The poor woman had gone pale in a millisecond, and was lucky that Jack had walked in at the right time. Pearl made a note to keep a good thought, and resumed the regular chores of lab maintenance, and spiffing the place up for visitors. Touching the handle of the cleaning cart, she felt the first vibration. Just a faint tingle, then a pause and another at lower frequency but higher amplitude, like a bone drawn across a tuning fork. She was familiar with the many pings, thumps and chimes transmitted by the pier's steel pilings, but this was the first one she could feel in her feet. The distant sound reminded her of the droning pipes in an Irish dirge. Pearl visualized Neptune playing cello with a fishbone.

She began to sense a rhythm in the sound, and was momentarily transfixed. The notes had given her the notion, with no sense of magic or mystery attached, that the song was meant for her alone. So she stopped to listen, then began to dance. The tempo was a sort of slow waltz, or a walking blues played with a slide on an electric bass, and she danced around the lab with a mop, well aware that the music was in her head alone. But that it nonetheless required movement, as she did a shuffling boogie to the captive audience of sea creatures in attendance. She felt fine. Groovin'.

· · ·

Dugan rolled the Ducati into his garage, grabbed the tank bag and headed inside still wearing his jacket and helmet, in the quick-step of nature's call. The Groucho crouch minimized the bladder pressure. Relieved, he threw his riding gear on the couch, removed his boots and went to the refrigerator for a beer. The compressor motor in the old Frigidaire seemed louder than usual.

An Angel City IPA in hand, he raised the kitchen window shade to reveal the true source of the humming sound. He was looking directly into the fish-eye lens of a camera affixed to the bottom of a four-rotor helicopter drone, about six feet from his face. Without putting down the beer, he bent slowly at the knees, opened slowly the cabinet door below the sink, and removed the .45 from its hook. There was always one in the chamber.

Rising again slowly, he simultaneously slid the window open with the thumb of his beer hand, raised the weapon and fired into the lens. Curiously, although the aircraft was knocked back about ten feet and wobbled slightly, it was still flying. And before he could get off another round, it banked upward sharply and disappeared to the north. As his surprise subsided, Dugan realized that firing toward the beach might not be the best choice anyway.

Who in the hell would have him under surveillance? Now he'd have to go through the house for bugs and cameras. Wilco Tango Foxtrot indeed. On the off-chance the operator was in sight, Dugan grabbed the brass telescope from the window sill and scanned the beach. Nothing, until he swept to the pier, where two men in suits were struggling with a control box as the drone circled the shoreline. Control was not remotely theirs, as the mini-chopper flew under the pier and appeared to strafe two children and a dog, then shot straight up, spiraling into the sun until the motors quit and it stalled, hung momentarily and dropped into the ocean. A hungry pelican followed it in, bound to be disappointed.

The suits ran for the beach, children were screaming and running, and the whole scene was quite entertaining. This would make a good video itself, Dugan thought. And who wears suits in Pismo? When he looked back again at the pier, sure enough there was young Mark with a camera in his hand, following the action. Some days you get the elevator.

He replaced the pistol under the sink and noticed the phone light blinking. A single message from Jack. *Hey, first thing to do when you get back is check in on Gina. She had a big fright yesterday and could use some help. Lemme know how she's keeping. Hope you had a good ride.*

Good to be home, Dugan thought, collected his riding gear and headed back to the garage. The going was getting strange, but could always be worse. Mid-October, 72 degrees outside. He could be in Cleveland.

· · ·

When she heard Dugan's motorcycle Gina was sitting at the kitchen table, which was spread with folders and papers. The sound prompted the notion that she might have put on makeup rather than making a gin-and-tonic, but as quickly thought oh what the fuck. If he shows up unannounced, he might know I wasn't expecting company. Not that it wasn't welcome.

"Hey," he said. "Someone play an early Halloween trick on you?" She attempted a smile by couldn't complete the circuit. Her bloodshot eyes began filling with tears, with her first admission out loud, "My son is AWOL, and probably under investigation by the CIA."

Dugan's incredulity, seriously taxed only minutes earlier, paused to add another debit. He noted the official-looking stamps on the folders in front of her, charting an ascending scale of consequences for their unauthorized viewing. "Tell you what, why don't you take your drink and I'll take these, and we'll go outside and talk." He could sweep the house for electronic monitors later, now it was time to move. Gina seemed glad for the direction.

He stacked the half-dozen paperwork files at right angles, secured a bottle of Sierra Nevada Torpedo from the refrigerator, and followed her sagging shoulders out the door. The picnic table sat in a triangulation of redwoods out back, a little Big Sur. He re-arranged the papers and sat, as Gina told him about the message from Rick, and handed him the note from Leon. He read it twice to make sure.

The tribal name of Jack's artist friend came to mind. This shit was getting entirely too serious. Dugan took a moment to put what he knew of Gina's information assault into some organized form, in the hope of making a plan. Failing that, as the silence lengthened, he said, "What did you say about Edward Snowden?"

"His name came up in Rick's message, but that's all I caught. There may be something in these files. Jesus, I just hope he doesn't end up in Russia."

"Okay, it looks like this happened quickly, whatever it was, and Leon was out the door at the first sign of trouble. I don't think you're even on the radar yet, but that's probably gonna be temporary. So I think we should go through this stuff, then decide what to do with it. And the best time to do that is now."

Ready for any help at all, Gina agreed. Dugan didn't mention his recent anti-aircraft engagement, since she already had plenty on her table, literally. And it wasn't material to be browsing when the feds arrived. Which gave him another pause. Maybe they shouldn't look at this stuff at all, just torch everything, disclaim any knowledge whatsoever. Or, on the other hand, pack it all up and stash it somewhere safe. Could come in handy as evidence if the whole deal wound up in a courtroom. But… evidence that would serve whom, the defense or the prosecution?

The looming potential for a real shitstorm clouded his thinking. The ping-pong of possibilities played on in his brain, when it was interrupted by the sound of a motorcycle in the driveway. "Stay put," he said, entered the house quickly and reached the front door as the rider arrived, still wearing his helmet. "I was asked to deliver this to Mrs. Brennan," he said, holding up a small plastic object.

"What is it?" Dugan asked

"Looks like a flash drive," said the helmet. "Is she here?"

"Indisposed at the moment, but I'll make sure she gets it. Is it from Leon?"

"Couldn't say." He handed it over, and the helmet swiveled. "That your Ducati?"

"It is."

"Cool." His gloved hand flashed a peace sign. His bike sat idling in the driveway. "Ride safe," he said, turned and motored away.

Twenty-Five

When Mark walked into Harry's, the Shrubbies were all but giddy in celebration. The silent TV screen showed two framed faces being co-interviewed. The names posted below showed a Karl Rove on the left and a Newt Gingrich on the right.

"It's the official Pinchmug Cabinet!" explained one. "That's Kent Ham on the left and Porky the Smirk on the right, the twin peaks of the Pinch clan food chain."

Mark could see that Henry was trying to get his attention at the other end of the bar, but he had to ask. "Well, the Pinchmugs are characterized by tiny faces in the middle of large heads. Their biological classification is unclear, maybe some sort of sub-species, or an unknown genetic disorder. Some have suggested fetal-alcohol syndrome, and the possibility of late-onset encephalitis is under study. But the condition is widespread." Mark attempted an expression of polite interest. "Any others I might recognize?"

"Well, there's Limbaugh of course, aka Toady the Wart, and Hannity and Scarborough. The Irish and Germans have contributed the most members in our country, but the syndrome spans cultures, Kim Jong Un as an example."

"What about O'Reilly," Mark asked.

"Ahh, Philo Smugly! Secretary of the Inferior. A borderline case, in terms of Pinchmuggery, but certainly in the same cerebral category. We count all the sideshow carnies as another great benefit of democracy. That notoriety is available to one and all, including the feeble-minded."

Mark's political menu extended only to what he hoped looked like real interest in the subject, and was glad to see Henry waving him to the back. "Hey, Byrnes said to give you a message, about some video you shot on the pier this morning."

"How did he know about that?"

"He's the one who disabled the drone. Said it's important for your own safety that you don't tell anyone about the video, or show it to anyone. Said he'd explain later."

The memory of the machine gun jellyfish had yet to erase itself from Mark's own mental archive, and childhood dreams of being devoured by giant sea creatures had recently resurfaced, so to speak. Thus a caution from Mr. Byrnes carried some resonance. So the decision to cancel his previously scheduled meeting with a TV reporter came with relative ease.

Mark could afford no difficulties with his father-in-law, whose continuing generosity was the only thing keeping his business afloat. There was no reason to implicate the hotel in anything that might turn out to be… suspicious, right? Nonetheless, he made back-up copies of all his videos on a hard drive that was safely hidden away. What Byrnes might have to do with the radio-controlled helicopter, and the Laurel and Hardy scene on the pier, was anybody's guess. The guy seemed to get involved in some weird shit, but he paid the bill.

Plus there was Henry's endorsement, what the hell… Mark found his own decisiveness quite pleasing, worthy at least of a beer and some popcorn, when his attention was consumed, all but devoured really, by the entrance of the most beautiful woman he'd ever seen.

· · ·

Spence and Jenny walked into Harry's together, noticed Pearl at the bar talking to a young man who appeared to have just seen a fellow owl, and took a table by the bandstand. The sight of Jenny hustled Henry over promptly.

"Hi," she smiled. "Who's that Pearl is talking to?"

"That's Mark." Henry said. "The video guy, lives next door, his father-in-law owns this place now."

"Is he breathing?" asked Spence.

They regarded Mark over Pearl's shoulder. He seemed to be caught in a tractor beam, frozen in a hypnotic state. "Hard to know," Henry replied. "I've heard that some humans carry amphibian characteristics, like they can breathe through their skin." Jenny gave Henry the you kidding? look, but he remained deadpan as usual. She asked him to tell Pearl they were there, which brought a smile and, "always a pleasure, miss." Henry had a lovely smile.

Spence asked about the magazine story, and Jenny admitted it was still pending. "I guess it's on hold," she said. Her research hadn't turned up anything of substance, but she'd heard about the helicopter drone and wondered if there could be a lead there. The meeting with Byrnes should give her some sense of whether the whole assignment was worth the bother. Then Pearl arrived with young Mark in tow.

"Hi, you two. This is Mark, he's a videographer and he has an underwater camera. I was telling him about your story, and Spence's work. He's offered to help out."

Mark, barely able to take his eyes off Pearl, explained that he could set up the camera and monitor a diver's video from a boat, and offer some direction, but couldn't enter the water himself. "I don't have a problem with lakes and rivers, but being in the ocean gives me the willies. I'm not sure why."

His apparent aquaphobia was outside the frame of reference for Spence and Pearl, but Jenny was sympathetic. Though not without noticing that Mark did present a rather frog-like appearance, and recalling that most of that species were less than fond of saltwater.

"We definitely appreciate your help," she said. "We haven't come up with much of anything so far." Mark asked if Pearl would be piloting the boat. "That would likely be my job," came the voice of Hank, who had appeared silently behind them. "I figure she and Spence would be in the water with cameras, since he's the pro diver and Pearl is our resident sea-nymph."

The word nymph gave Mark a twinge in his nethers. She turned to Hank. "Mark says he can rig an underwater camera you can see on a laptop in the boat, so it would be like Face Time. At which Hank smiled and Pearl seem to blush, in a fashion, as if they had a different definition of the term. Then Henry punched up the sound system, with a gumbo-shuffle groove by Paul Brady, and the couple had the dance floor to themselves.

> There ain't no happy time without no pain,
> heartbreak, new date, move on up the alleyway
> Pick up them pieces hit the road again, uh huh, uh huh
> The world is what you make it
> The world is what you make it baby
> The world is what you make it

Mark was transfixed by Pearl's movements, as if her flowing motions belonged to some archetypal creature of the sea, her hair floating in rhythm, the contours of her muscular legs and torso re-affirming his abiding wonderment at the astounding beauty of women. In his trance, the arrival at the bar of Dugan Byrnes and Jack Padilla went unnoticed.

Henry sat a pint of Barrelhouse IPA in front of Dugan, and a Firestone Pils for Jack, who was driving. "The young folks have been chattering away about something," he said. "I take it you guys have set up a meeting."

"That's a true fact," Byrnes replied, not surprised that Henry kept a finger on the pulse of neighborhood activity. "We're going to compare notes, and Pearl's giving us a tour of the Poly lab tomorrow. We're thinking of putting together some sort of baywatch volunteer group, so we can monitor what's going on."

"I'm sure Mark would volunteer to film Pearl running on the beach," Henry said. "In fact, if you need any extras..."

"Not that sort of baywatch, Henry," Jack said. "Just a rotating crew of monitors."

"Shit, who wants to look at the ocean all day," replied Henry, pausing slightly to recall having done exactly that a few times himself. "You could just check the recordings every day from that video weather service, they have cameras all along the coast that just show the surf all day long. The wide angle covers the whole bay."

Dugan registered another marker of respect for Henry, his ability to think when he wasn't getting paid, and waved Jack to join him with the group he hoped to volunteer. He was a bit surprised to see Spence among them, and recognized Jenny, the winsome journalist who had coveted his jacket. The two younger people were unfamiliar, but he figured the blonde lad who looked like a Beach Boys roadie had to be Hank, and that his raven-haired companion would be Pearl. Jack was right, she certainly was something to look at.

After Jenny made the necessary introductions, Dugan suggested moving their meeting to the beach where it would be quieter. Consensus came quickly, and they headed the few hundred feet to the shore.

Twenty-Six

None among the entourage could be aware of the notice given their procession by an entity at the end of the pier. She had made some connection with most of them individually, without their knowledge, but two stood out as the most receptive humans; the young girl with darker skin and the older fellow they called Dugan, who was apparently a leader. How she had arrived at these perceptions, indeed how she had achieved consciousness itself, remained unknown to her. She was aware that her size far exceeded the average scale of her species, that she had somehow absorbed considerable physical and mental powers, and that she had recently been assigned a name by someone among the land creatures. She was called Edna, an acronym somehow related to the effects of electromagnetic radiation and DNA, which comprised her current course of study. Learning had become her way of life, in the implicit sense that knowledge was a genetic necessity. But self-awareness was a more mystifying set of questions, having no counterpart among her species with whom she could share and collaborate. One of one.

Edna was aware of her singularity, and, so far as she knew, her singularly large scale. Her current stage allowed speeds to keep pace with the fastest creatures in the ocean, the ability to move below the sand, and the capacity to empathize with aquatic animals of other species, and to communicate with them. Merely by concentration she could generate powerful electrical signals, and receive, decode when necessary, and file information sent via land, sea or air. With the classified information, once she got through the algorithms, the encryption was relatively easy. Edna loved math, and the music of the homo-sapiens.

She had not, to her knowledge, ever been seen by any of the humans. Which had seemed necessary for some reason, the notion that to reveal herself too soon held the prospect of injury to innocents among them, or to herself for that matter. She felt strongly the conviction that allies would be necessary. She understood that her mission, assigned by a source unknown, was that of messenger. Edna recognized that mutations (knowing she was one), can produce global consequences of the life-threatening kind. She considered her job description signal bearer, sent to warn the land-form species of their impending peril. Thus far she had befriended the jellyfish, a squad of what she learned were larger-than-average frogs, and the dolphins – always a joy to the eyes and ears.

Over the years (37 human by her calculation), information had come to her from dry land largely in the form of electrical transmissions through the four large steel pipes running from the coast to the end of the Cal Poly pier. ("Better part of half a mile," she heard one visitor say.) Once used for oil shipment, the conduits now served as hard-wired connections to the coastline. Before that she had discovered the fiber-optic cables coming ashore nearby, a voluminous source of data from around the world. From Morro Bay to Vandenberg, the coastline was a focal nexus of global communication.

She had grown to size in a data rich environment, but one also flush with contaminants. She came to perceive the irony. With the pier as a huge horizontal antenna, Edna also had access to satellite signals from everywhere. And with the unexpected arrival of the container called Leona Philpot (from a company named Microsoft, which she would learn was neither small nor spongy), her education would be complete. The submerged data cylinder also gave her a WiFi connection to Pearl's computer in the lab, which added another tutorial in the arts of encryption. Her education seemed to be proceeding nicely.

The data covering her own lifespan was simple enough to absorb and consider, the previous half-century proving far more complex and curious. By the time she got to the Great war, an introduction to what was called the Second World, her faith in the land form species was sorely strained. The intermission between wars had apparently provided the time to build more and better weapons and sell them. Once the competing national and ethnic groups chose up sides, the killing began in earnest and lasted five years, until her future home-land had dropped two atomic bombs, beginning the Atomic Age. Which would become the Electronic Age, in what had come to be called the American Century.

Edna found it all instructive, but it naturally created more ques-tions, the foremost being how, after the massive death and destruc-tion of two wars, could they have not called it settled. Okay then, done deal. But the appeals of more industry, jobs and wealth were so enticing that the larger nations, as they called them, would keep the ball rolling with proxy wars. Which brought her local and world history file up to date. Still, with same game plan remaining in effect, the question remained. Why?

Close as she could come, given what seemed little time for extensive research, and pushing out to the limits of deduction, was to identify the two most prominent causative factors as alcohol and nicotine. Either one, when not combined with the other, could pose real problems, but combined often led to disaster. Even alcohol and intelligence blended just so could produce periods of galloping dis-orientation, and acts of genuine stupidity. Which naturally generated the next why, what was it about alcohol?

Without getting too far into the brain chemistry, on which doc-umentation was surprisingly scant, she concluded that it came down to the drug's effect: Permission. Alcohol, nicotine and a number of other chemical stimulants, apparently gave humans the notion to do whatever they wanted, without regard for their own or other species. And that the best way to induce them to do so was to prohibit the substance. With the result that, by the end of the Second World kill-ings, a number of pickled smokers had come to power in Washing-ton, D.C. Their biochemistry, also affected by doses of lead, iodine, mercury, arsenic, nitrates and natural and man-made radiation, pro-duced decisions that would not only perpetuate the national warfare system, but also accelerate the capacity for the species' self-extinc-tion.

The motives for collective destruction and death, greed and revenge, remained in place as they had for centuries. But the weap-onry had improved immensely, as had the market. Perhaps, she thought, the humanoids were merely aping their ancestors. Acting on a primal gene that required tribal battles for territory and food, but which now necessitated modifying their brain chemistry to activate the impulse. She was reluctant to extend the formula to the conclusion that their history of bloodlust had rendered the homo sapiens self-made mutants. But it was apparent that their current state of political discourse was dangerously polluted.

Edna regretted the incident with the man on the fishing boat, but the clattering beer bottles when she was trying to sleep had pro-voked her temper. She reckoned that his elimination (as humans called it) had been necessary, and that the earth was likely no worse for his absence. But there was that note of remorse at his death. A twinge, as the humans said. She had been watching reruns of Barney Miller from Pearl's computer. "Yes your honor," she would plead in court. "I did feel a twinge of remorse."

Nonetheless, as she'd heard one lander remark, consciousness is a bitch. She was pleased that her most recent allies, the jellyfish, had agreed to deliver the little metal object the man had used to make noise and kill. And to find she had the support of the frog-men, who had also experienced physical and mental changes in their species. She was somehow gaining cooperation from other inhabitants of the ocean. Edna knew she was an anomaly in her own species, but no longer felt alone.

The jellyfish were lovely and helpful, and she loved their singing, far softer than the whales but also wonderful. (They also looked good enough to eat, but she put the thought aside.) The frog-men were strong and fast, and the dolphins! She had learned to swim at their speed for short distances, leaping and playing. When her electromagnetic thrust ran low, four of them would carry her just above the surface, and it was thrilling to ride in the wind. She understood the humans' love of surfing. She imagined what it must be like to ride a motorcycle.

But her new friends also brought reports of other species' mutations in the ocean, some with bad intent. Edna wasn't pleased to imagine an octopus twice her size. She had gained the attention of the humans who appeared sympathetic, the decision now was what to do with it.

Twenty-seven

The only others on the beach were a few surfers gathering their gear, about to douse the low fire in a pit. Dugan hailed and asked them to let it burn, and his group settled in around the fading glow, the lingering flames dancing in a light breeze from the southwest. The sun had set without flashes of any color, the marine layer floating a half-mile offshore, obscuring the horizon.

"Okay," Dugan addressed the collective. "Some of you know each other and a few have just met. Let's go around the circle, introduce ourselves, and report our experiences. See if we can come up with a bigger picture."

Jenny outlined her magazine assignment, and growing frustration with what little tangible information she had found. "I'm hoping someone here can provide something more to go on," she said. "Right now I'm researching the nature and level of chemical pollution in the ocean, and the causes of recent algae blooms and their effects on sea life and the fisheries. Solid facts are hard to come by from the bureaucrats, but based on what I'm hearing from you folks, something else is clearly going on out there."

Hank recounted his extended surfboard ride on the random wave from nowhere, and having heard similar stories from a few other surfers. "No idea what's creating them," he said. "I like to think they're just little gifts from the ocean." Spence then covered his admittedly vague mission from Scripps, and his puzzlement over the row of shallow divots along the pier. "It looks like a 30-foot wide soup ladle scooped them out at regular intervals. Stronger wave action fills them back in, but a few days later they reappear. I turned in my photos at the institute, but have yet to hear any results or theories."

Dugan leaned over and whispered to Mark that they might want to keep the topic of armed jellyfish to themselves for the time being. Producing a computer tablet, Mark related his video shoot of the drone and the two suits with the controller, as the scene made its way around the circle, accompanied by chuckles. "I ran out of battery when the pelicans arrived," he said. "I looked through my bag and couldn't find a spare, so I headed back to the studio. When I got to the Cool Cat I looked back and a Coast Guard cutter had already arrived, and a diver was going over the side."

Jack gave a summary of his bay search with Dugan, omitting the machine gun, but including the tale of diver Hector Romero's alleged switch in skin pigmentation, noting that it remained unverified. Then Pearl delivered a quick synopsis of her role at the marine lab, and a halting but lyrical account of her passionate feelings about the ocean, and that acidification and heat appeared to be the most probable cause in the recent loss of fisheries. Spence and Mark were completely attentive. "But yesterday," she continued, "I had the strangest experience. In the middle of regular chores, I started hearing musical notes. Not audibly, the vibrations came through my hands and feet."

"What tune was it?" asked Hank.

"Nothing I'd heard before, just a series of tones that had a rhythm, and it felt somehow that … that it was a song just for me, that I was the audience of one. And I started dancing around the lab with a mop."

By now Mark and Spence were transfixed by their own visuals, and after a collective pause Jack said, "That sounds pretty magical." With nods all around.

Dugan's synopsis of his coastal ride noted his meeting with Simon and Gus, that the result may soon grace their company with the use of a two-place submarine, and that the three men had seen a video clip showing what they agreed appeared to be a giant frog in Monterey Bay. Which produced another brief silence.

He then mentioned Gina's son's former job at Vandenberg,

omitting the specifics, and asked if she'd found anything in Leon's papers. "Most of it's too technical for me," she said. "But it's clear that our government has a big stake in the surveillance business. Way more than just phone and email records in this country, they have ears in all the business and government communications on the planet. And there was a detailed tracking chart of Russian and Chinese submarine routes in the Pacific, and some stuff on the Baltic Sea. But for our group this little item jumped out, so I'll read it to you. It looks like a copy of a memo, the heading is just Miscellaneous: NASA Satellite Images."

> At the direction of DOD, in joint effort with the FBI, CIA, NSA,
> DEA and NOAA, we have observed and recorded images of
> a mobile object in the Pacific Ocean just off the central coast
> of California. Manned/Unmanned/Manner of Control:
> Undetermined. The object, which generally moves at approximately
> five to seven knots for short distances, has also been timed at
> sustained speeds of up to 40 knots until out of range; it appears
> at varying depths and often just 10 to 20 feet below the surface.
> The object is roughly ovoid with one side partially flattened.
> The estimated diameter is 36 feet; section depth and weight
> unknown. Material composition undetermined. Manner of
> propulsion unknown. Report based on three independent sightings.
> Investigation continuing.

Dugan's first notion was to wonder if this meeting was being recorded from outer space, his second to ask Gina the date on the document. His assumption that if it was more than a few weeks past, the Navy would already have active underwater surveillance on site. He made a note to check in with Jimmie Burke in D.C. for any under-counter leads, and considered coming forth with the jellyfish sighting. Things were getting interesting.

But before he could ask her the question, Byrnes caught a movement in the fire, now just down to embers. The topmost chunk was turning ashen, and began to dissolve and slide down the sides, but simultaneously appeared to leave a glowing green ball at the top. Which also seemed to be rising quite slowly above the fire. He looked to see if any of his seven companions were seeing the same thing. All were looking at the luminous baseball-sized sphere.

The narrative of what happened next would vary with each member of the group, though all agreed how it began. Their eyes had closed together, arms rising slowly on both sides, their hands clasping those of their neighbors. And each would recall the sensation that the sand beneath them lifted slightly with the rise of the green globe, that they were floating just above the beach. But each of the eight experienced his and her own event, though all agreed that it had definitely qualified as an expansion of conscious. Or an introduction to another form thereof.

Curiously, only Dugan retained a memory of the conclusion, while the others recalled only the feeling of waking up from a nap, which included a dream of some substance. As he returned to regular time and space, his eyes opened to see those of the others still closed, their hands still connected. The green glow was gone, the fire just gray ash. His eyes fell on Hank, wearing what could be called a beatific smile, who then began to sing, the others joining in.

Letting the days go by, let the water hold me down
Letting the days go by, water flowing underground
Into the blue again, after the money's gone
Once in a lifetime, water flowing underground

Same as it ever was... Same as it ever was...
Same as it ever was... Same as it ever was...
Water dissolving... and water removing

There is water at the bottom of the ocean
Under the water, carry the water at the bottom of the ocean
Remove the water at the bottom of the ocean

The harmony was stirring, the song becoming a communal chant that carried along the shore, ending as their hands parted and eyes opened, smiling. At which Dugan became aware of his own breathing, recognized his familiar if limited grasp on consciousness, and realized that none gathered here would likely ever again see the world the same as they ever had.

Twenty-Eight

Henry was going through the bar order when his feet started tingling. He recalled the similar sensation with the regular arrival of a squadron of weekend outlaws on Harleys rumbling down Pomeroy Avenue, blipping their throttles and backing in to the curb. Similar but somehow different, and much quieter. Then the liquor bottles on the shelves began to clink and rattle, and the lights reflected in the mirrored walls jittered. Harry's was enclosed in a low-frequency hum, as if it had been plugged into a bass amplifier, which passed through in a few seconds and was gone.

The bar was nearly empty at sundown, one couple at a table and old Gladys nursing a gin and tonic and watching the silent TV monitor. At her familiar snort Henry looked up to see the flushed face of the current leader in the auditions for the Republican presidential nomination. His erratic gestures and self-aggrandizing oration suggested either cocaine or some prescription drug for attention deficit disorder. His coloring indicated a beta-carotene overdose. While the shrubbies had yet to determine his Pinchmug status, entries for his nom-de-plumage included the Tangerine Dweeb, the Florid Feuhrer, and Byrnes' favorite, Donnie the Mook. Gladys had her own title, the Amber Panderer. Henry offered up the Marmalade Mouthbreather. But it was quiet Herb Tuttle who claimed the honors with the Apricot Apoplectic.

"My brother-in-law went to military boarding school with him," Gladys said. "Just another trust-fund asshole, he said, but plenty of bluster and an ego that far outweighed his abilities. The cheerleaders liked him."

Henry didn't know much about Gladys's background, only that she was maybe ten years older than him, generally kindhearted, and regarded as one of the local hippie pioneers. "I think Trump has provided a great public service," she said, "just for showing how far the police state has come since 1968. That's when we almost got representative democracy back, but the Democrats caved, and instead we got a paranoid drunk who invaded Cambodia. That's when the plutocrats really got a foothold."

"Yeah, but they lost," Henry said.

"Sure, they lost Vietnam, then blamed it on Johnson and dismissed any culpability. But they extended the life span of their sustaining communist bogeyman, the so-called cold war. And even though they lost to the Democrats, and watched the dreaded nuclear threat recede, by the time they installed Reagan, the 'acting president', they had almost run out of commies. Of course then they took credit for destroying the Soviet Union.

"You know Reagan, the Bushes and Trump don't have much in common in terms of character and personality, but they do share the common denominator of simplemindedness. Trump just brings more entertainment to the sideshow, as a carny who manages to combine all the ugliest national character traits in a continuous eruption of venal bigotry, narcissism and sociopathic invective. He's the toady, barker, ringmaster and animal trainer all in one. For awhile he even had Sarah Palin as the bearded lady. His act reminds me of a novel I read back in the day," she said.

"What was it called?" Henry asked.

"A Confederacy of Dunces," she said. "I know they say you can't fix stupid, but it doesn't mean you have to elect it president."

"Gladys, allow me to buy you a drink."

. . .

As Henry returned to his paperwork the phone rang. "Hello, this is Gus Martin. I've been trying to get hold of Dugan Byrnes, with no luck. He told me this would be a good place to leave a message."

"That's a true fact," Henry replied. "What can I tell him?"

"Just that Clamentine is good to go, and we're ready to put her in shallow water for a test dive. He said that he could help with a good place to put in. The weather and tides look good, so we should be in Pismo by this weekend."

"I'll pass it on when he comes in."

"Thanks, is this Henry?"

"'Tis."

"I hear you're the world's best bartender."

"Also a true fact." Hanging up, he turned to find Norman Valentine, owner of the novelty shop across the street, seated at the bar. "Was that an earthquake?" he asked.

"Either that or Mark had some real audio mix-up next door," Henry said. "That kid has a whole wall of serious amps and speakers. Maybe he plugged in the wrong thing."

"No, I just saw him down at the beach with a group of people. Looked like they'd shared some mushrooms or something, singing around a campfire. My dog was howling, in the right key. I think it was G major."

Henry remembered that Norman played cello in the local symphony orchestra. "Was Byrnes with them?" Norman nodded just as Mark walked in, trailed by Jack and Gina. While Halloween was still a few weeks off, each appeared to be practicing their own zombie expressions. The thousand-yard stare that seemed to see something in the future. Zoned.

"You guys okay?" Henry asked.

The threesome smiled simultaneously, their eyes coming slowly into focus, and said in unison, "We've been down at the beach." Which also caught the attention of Norman and Gladys, as Henry puzzled over the possibilities. Had they witnessed an accident? Gotten some bad news? Or some good drugs?

Then Jack said, "A round for the house!" and found no dissent-

157

ers. At which Dugan came through the side door on Cypress Street and said, "How lovely!" An expression none had ever heard him use before.

. . .

The conversation that followed would also come to be recalled in various ways over the following years, the facts sliding about, shifting in accuracy and description, the shadowed halls of recollection producing considerable ambiguation. Their collective memory would become a dense patch of disparate shrubbery, full of dramatic incidents and convoluted tales of intrigue. Mention would be made of a possible movie.

But for the present tense, the individuals (later dubbed *The Pismo Eight* by the media) came to acknowledge that each had been enlisted by an unknown force of some kind to perform as yet undesignated tasks for the common good. And that details were forthcoming. The remaining members of the group straggled in, gradually reestablishing a bond with linear reality through small talk and alcohol, and slowly convened around the pool table.

"So," Dugan began, "it seems we've just shared an experience that was, uh… outside the standard conceptual framework, with some elements common to the group and others specific to each individual."

"How do you know that?" asked Spence.

"No idea. But I can tell you that when I opened my eyes, when the song had ended and the green light was gone, all of you still had your eyes closed. Which I have interpreted, for some reason, to mean that I had been selected as an observer. That I was supposed to retain some sort of objective overall picture of the event. And that's when we stopped holding hands."

"We were singing and holding hands?" Mark asked. "That's interesting," Pearl said. "So, if you have been appointed secretary of this … whatever it is… what did you take away that we should all know?"

"Well, I've been thinking about that on the walk, and when I finish this glass of beer, will endeavor to answer as best I can." Following a toast to their unexpected pact, and a buzz of questions among the group, Byrnes began.

"My impressions are still taking shape," he said. "But I think we've somehow been collectively introduced to a new form of intelligence, and were chosen for a reason. That it's a living organism which wants to inform us of something, and that it's not a threat. I feel it wanted our attention in order to pass on some wisdom that we needed to have. Why I don't know. And, this was the epilogue, that when this message had been imparted, did we have any questions?"

Head-scratching looks were exchanged, short-term memories scanned. "I can remember two," he went on. "I simply asked what do you want? And the reply was, 'we need your help.' So I said who is we? 'All of us, the living beings in the water and on the land, including you', was the answer."

Byrnes now had their attention. Expressions evolved to show the dawning glimmer of recovered information, an unknown known. Hmm. "And what was the second question," asked Gina, smiling as if she already knew.

"What is your name?" Dugan replied.

At which enlightenment settled like a comic strip balloon over the Pismo Eight, who raised their glasses and cheered in unison, "Edna!"

Twenty-Nine

Each of The Eight agreed it was good to know they had a new friend, despite the cosmic weirdness of their encounter, and all were keen to discover who, or what, she was. Everyone realized that their respective missions had been transposed from investigation to collaboration, and that each now possessed a voluminous file of data on the changing conditions in the ocean. The troublesome certainty that there was real cause for alarm, and that something had to be done. A little knowledge…

By the next day Dugan found himself unusually comfortable as appointed group captain, albeit apprehensive about what the responsibility might entail. While management roles had rarely suited him, the rule of thumb that forgiveness was usually more easily obtained than permission had served well enough through the years. "I don't see any need for command decisions," he told Jack. "It seems we all have our assignments, and we can likely expect another communication as things shake out. Whoever or whatever we're dealing with apparently has a plan."

They had convened on his deck, over glasses of New Belgium Citricum IPA, awaiting the arrival of Gina and Gloria with pizza. "Reckon you're right," Jack said. "I know that with the possible exception of one especially illuminating acid trip, that was the most… uh, arresting mental experience on my score card. Like a surrealistic dream that leaves a lasting impression, but one you're unable to explain. Which reminds me, you remember that dream I mentioned the other day, when Gloria and I realized we'd both had the same one?"

"I do, been waiting for you to tell me about it."

"It was quite absorbing," he said. "We were underwater, freediving, but not together. And we both swam into some sort of… festival,

I suppose you could call it, with maybe a dozen creatures in a kind of ritual dance. They were leaping and spinning in some fantastical choreography, in slow motion. It was captivating. And we both saw the same performance, dig, in our own dreams."

"What did the creatures look like?" Dugan asked.

"Humanoid. And *caballus*. Maybe a dozen men and women on horseback, nude, and perfectly formed in both species, and almost integrated into one being. Equus-Homo sapien. The word beautiful falls way short."

Dugan had the momentary vacancy expression, known to those who are headed rapidly south when they're suddenly confronted by the backside of a northbound shovel.

"Holy freakin' cowbell," he said.

"We could always use more cowbell," said Jack.

"Looks like we got it."

· · ·

Spence knew he had to head back to La Jolla right after the clam festival, with no clear way in mind to report his experience to Getz. Then realized he was off duty anyway, so no worries. He'd been assured by his mystical collaborator on the beach that the sand divots along the pier were hers. That she meant no harm, was no threat to national security, and would fill him in later. He had also acquired a bibliography of reference material on chemical reactions, radiation and genetic mutations. And the comfort of knowing that he and Byrnes were actually on the same side.

Jenny had been furnished a detailed outline of an extraordinary story, Pulitzer stuff, also with a list of references, and the suggestion to hire a good photographer. Mark was now all but convinced that no harm would come to him in the ocean, and became fixed on the image of Pearl swimming underwater, and the performance art his video could present to the world.

For her part, Pearl had experienced a profoundly emotional connection with what was obviously a non-human being. She could only equate the feeling with the reverence and respect she felt for her own mother. She had always known a strong kinship with the ocean, now it seemed reciprocal. Hank was pleased to know the source of his everlasting wave, and the background fact that he and fellow surfers had at first been mistaken for dolphins, who also enjoyed the long rides.

Gina took comfort in the reassurance that her son was safe, that he would return unharmed, and wasn't likely to be court-martialed. Everyone wondered what might come next. As a group, they'd been advised to avoid any phone or email communications, to meet only in person and in the open. All had been exposed to some measure of surveillance, and Gina had drawn the most federal interest.

With the confirmation that Gus and his submersible would arrive two days hence, the next group meeting was set for Avila Beach, the least conspicuous place to put in without attracting undue attention. And provide quick access to the Cal Poly pier. Plus a congested roadway to hinder pursuit should a swift escape be required.

Alternate routes would fall to Jack's panga boat, now fitted with a powerful V8 and a modified hull, which could easily outpace anything in the Coast Guard fleet, except the radio. Hank would handle the four-place Zodiac, courtesy of Cal Poly, with Pearl and Spence suited to dive, and Mark with his full video kit. The mission was twofold – to observe and record any activity in the water, and to shepherd Clamantine's shakedown dive, and make sure she got back to shore.

. . .

"That makes it threefold," Gina said. "And this is a three-cheese pizza with mushrooms, olives, artichoke hearts and bits of prosciutto." Gloria cleared the deck table and added a growler of Coast Brewing IPA and four glasses, as the elders of the Pismo Eight conspired to enjoy the food and company. The unseasonably strong winds, nudging hurricane force in the afternoon, had subsided. But their severity had closed the dunes to vehicular traffic, and posted health warnings for Oceano and the Nipomo mesa. Now a not quite full moon shimmered on calm water, a thin marine layer gathered a mile offshore as stars sparkled in turn throughout the blue-black canopy of sky.

"Much as I hate to use the vernacular," Jack said, reaching for another slice, "this is totally awesome."

"Quite satisfactory," replied Dugan. "We may be needing the carbs. You guys should stay here tonight, no need to go to Santa Ynez and come back in the morning. And your boat's already here."

"Works for me," said Jack, with an inquiring look to Gloria. "We can do that," she said, "but I have to be back for an appointment on Saturday."

"And miss the Clam Festival?" Gina asked.

"Oh, easily. I've seen more than my share, was in one of the marching bands myself years ago. But I have other chores, and anyway, nobody makes better clam chowder than I do, she said modestly."

"Indisputably," said Dugan, lighting the gas fire pit in the middle of the deck. "What do you say we talk a bit about strategy for tomorrow? At least have a loose plan."

"You're going in the submersible, right?" Gina asked.

"Yeah, if it's cool with Gus. If not I'll go with Jack. So, he and Hank will flank the sub, and keep an eye on the surface. We'll all be in radio contact, so if you have an alert, mention it promptly. We want to get the sub out where we put in, but if that's not possible we need to rendezvous elsewhere. Fifteen minutes or so in the water should be plenty."

"Where will elsewhere be?" asked Gloria. "If I need to take the trailer to another spot."

"If it goes hinky out there," Dugan said, "which I don't think will happen, Jack will have to head north, Cayucos maybe. Hank can decide where he puts in, then we'll coordinate a meeting spot by radio. That said, it should be a piece of cake; we'll look like any other boaters on the water."

"Except for the drug smuggler boat," Gloria observed.

"Actually, Jack would be a good decoy," Dugan said. "They might concentrate on him, leave everyone else alone and end up finding nothing, no harm."

"So if we have to split," Jack said, "and the sub can't get to the loading ramp, where does it go?"

"There's a hiding spot in Pirate's Cove." replied Dugan.

"You can't get a trailer in there!" Jack said.

"I know. That's just the last resort scenario, where Gus's friend Simon calls in a helicopter. Of course we're hoping that won't be necessary."

"Let's drink to that," said Gina. As glasses clinked, the CD player shuffled to the next tune at random, and the foursome joined voices in their personal impressions of harmony.

> *In the town where I was born, lived a man who sailed the sea,*
> *And he told us of his life, in the land of submarines,*
> *So we sailed up to the sun, till we found a sea of green*
> *And we lived beneath the waves, in our yellow submarine*
> *We all live in a yellow submarine*
> *Yellow submarine, yellow submarine,*
> *We all live in a yellow submarine*
> *Yellow submarine, yellow submarine*

Thirty

Jack awoke spooned to Gloria's warm hindquarters, his arm around her torso and hand cupping her left breast, forefinger to the awakening nipple. "Is the sun also rising?" she whispered.

"Believe it is," he said, "but alas we must away to the beachhead for our class in advanced oceanography."

"I smell fresh tortillas and bacon. First things first."

Gina was cracking eggs at the stove when Dugan appeared. "I just talked to Gus, he's loading up. We'll pick him up at Sycamore Springs, Pearl and the boys are meeting us at the pier."

"Aye aye, captain. The coffee's ready, burritos in five minutes. Got an avocado?" Dugan headed for his secret stash in the garage when his phone rang. "Byrnes, hey it's Mike Sweeny at the station."

"Officer Mike!" he replied. "Been awhile, what's up with the Pismo PD?"

"Well, we've had some feds scratching around here, seem to be looking for drug smugglers, but that sounds fishy. Think it has something to do with that drone that crashed at the beach the other day. Anyway, your name came up in conversation and I wondered if you'd run into them."

"They haven't been by, " Dugan said. "Did they look like Mormons?"

"Now that you mention it…"

"Okay, I've heard about them, and do think the drug thing is a cover. Or somebody is pulling their chain. But just in case, my friend Jack has a panga boat and we're going fishing today at Avila, no contraband aboard. So if you hear from them, or the Coast Guard, you might just say no worries. Appreciate it."

"Not a problem, my friend. And let me know if you get any poop on these guys. We should get together again for coffee sometime."

"Look forward to it. Say, speaking of investigations, I heard that a couple of connected guys from Jersey were asking questions at Harry's, about a missing buddy."

"Yeah, they were here last week, filed a missing person's report. We haven't come up with anything so far, apparently he was on a fishing boat that was confiscated by the Coast Guard, and its owner is missing as well. The feds questioned him and he dropped off the screen. Probably witness protection."

"Heard about that, and the boat went to Vandenberg. Also hear the military down there has a missing person issue. Have they been in touch?"

"Ahh…, I'm afraid that's a locked file, my friend. But since we both know his mother, I gotta tell ya, that boy could be lookin' at some real bad paper and a hard road. Reckon he's likely out of country by now. Probably nothing you don't already know."

"Right, thanks Mike. She's collected a heavy load. Let's keep in touch."

. . .

Dugan didn't mention his conversation to Gina, figuring he'd go over it with her later, if at all. Nothing new to report. Pulling in to Sycamore Springs in Jack's truck, he spotted Simon of the Big South next to a nondescript enclosed trailer behind an old Ford van. Gus appeared as they came alongside.

"Good morning," Simon said. "Thought I'd join the party in case the electronics needed any troubleshooting."

"Cool deal." He introduced Simon and Gus to Gina, Jack and Gloria. "The rest of the crew is meeting us at the launch ramp just up the road. Are you riding shotgun in the sub?" he asked Simon.

"I'd rather be on the surface and monitor the video. Do you want to go down?"

"I purely do. In that case you can ride in Jack's boat, and we'll have radio contact between all three craft. And video if Mark's transmitter works."

"Clamantine has one on board," Gus said, "so we can have two feeds." He was eyeing the panga boat with interest. "Never saw one of those with hydrofoils before."

"It's a project," Jack said, "but she planes nicely if the chop isn't too nasty. I installed a good dose of horsepower in the process."

"What engine did you put in?" Gus asked.

"Just a small-block Chevy, out of a van about the same vintage as Simon's. But it has a few special parts and a blower, so she'll get up and honk." Gus looked reassured, and walked behind the trailer to have a look at the prop, noticing the red calligraphy on the transom.

Nipples
Pismo Beach, Calif.

At the shore, Pearl and Spence were suited up, she in her favorite purple wetsuit, checking their tanks as Mark loaded his video gear in the Zodiac, and Hank went through the safety check. Jack backed his trailer down the ramp as Dugan stood watch and signaled, and Gus pulled in parallel to the road. With the panga in the water, Jack and Dugan came up to help while Jenny stayed with the boat.

"I don't need the ramp," Gus said. "She's got her own dolly and we can just roll her down to the water." He dropped the tailgate ramp, released the tie-downs and with Simon on one side, rolled out the sub. Cradled between two bicycle frames with fat tires, Clamantine was revealed to the team of eight co-conspirators. Even in the morning overcast, her neon yellow Porsche hull brightened the beach. The group was speechless. "I know," Simon laughed. "It looks like the Jetsons have landed."

Gina smiled. "We have a yellow submarine."

"I'll be go to hell in hand basket," said Jack. "That is absofreakinlutely beautiful."

"Thanks," Gus replied. "Now we'll find out if she works properly." At the waterline, Hank, Dugan, Jack and Simon each took a corner and Gus pulled the dolly out. He popped the hatch on the Plexiglas dome and said, "Welcome aboard Mr. Byrnes, you are the first passenger and hopefully not the last."

"A hope we share," he said and climbed in. Gus pushed off, hopped in behind and secured the hatch, Clamantine bobbing in the rising tide like a lost space pod awaiting return of the mothership. Taking on ballast water, the waterline rose to the occupants' shoulder level, giving the bubble the visual effect of a giant jellyfish with two human heads for eyes.

Gus punched up the camera monitors, a four-screen panorama on the curved instrument panel. "Let's check our radios," he said. Jack and Simon checked in, then Hank and Pearl, followed by Gloria and Gina on the beach. Good to go. "Okay, we are operational," he said. "Your seat cushion is not your flotation device, nor will oxygen masks appear from overhead. If for some reason I'm disabled, pull that red handle by your left knee and we should float to the surface."

Dugan noted the first tentacles of apprehension sliding into his brain. "Copy that, captain." he said. "I trust that your capabilities will not be compromised. In fact, I'm counting on it."

He hadn't mentioned the group's mystical directive to either Gus or Simon, lacking any rational explanation and seeing no need to raise caution flags. Seemed their only potential danger would come in human form, mechanical failure notwithstanding.

"Okay," said Gus, "we are under power. We can stay on the surface for awhile and dive when we reach deeper water. You're the cruise director, got a course in mind?"

"Let's head for the end of Harford Pier, dead ahead, then backtrack on a tighter radius and come alongside the Poly Pier. That should give us a good scan on this side, then we can go around and down the other side, where Spence's divots are. Then sweep the Avila shoreline and head back in. If there's any issue at the ramp, we'll go on around to Pirate's Cove."

"Roger that, yer the navigator. We've got sixty feet here, ready to go under?"

"Dive, man!"

The fog was clearing off as the morning sun improved visibility, the temperature in the sub descended in kind, and the experimental human-controlled underwater vehicle was off to sea. Their radio handle, Winken and Blinken.

"Okay," Gus said, "we're at thirty-five feet and can see about the same distance. The cameras are actually more perceptive with all the lights up, so objects will appear on the screens a bit before we see them." At the Harford terminus sun and clear sky had doubled the visibility, but little of interest appeared in the water. The ocean floor was littered with fishing poles, baskets, T-shirts, coolers, the splintered hull of a Japanese fishing boat, a laptop computer, shopping cart, umbrellas, a complete 1968 Datsun 510, a few tents, hundreds of plastic soda bottles and a couple sea lion carcasses. An underwater junkyard in the shade. Clamantine shared the travel lanes with packets of perch, salmon and steelhead trout flashing in the oblique sunlight.

As they came about Dugan looked up to see Jack to starboard and the Zodiac opposite, slowly circling them on watch for kayakers, paddle boarders or the random dipshit on a jet ski. Nothing out of the ordinary showed along the shore, and approaching the foot of the Poly pier he could see Pearl and Spence go into the water. "Divers in," Hank reported. "We have them on-screen," Gus replied. "Following at forty feet, tell them to wave us in if we need a closer shot. You receiving our video?"

"Affirmative, roger wilco," Hank replied. "Always wanted to say that."

Thirty-One

Edna knew they were coming. She had picked up the radio signals when they launched, and was anxious to meet Dugan and Pearl face to face, so to speak. Their introduction on the beach had gone well, she seemed to have their trust, and the time had come to present her plan and confirm their commitment. And present herself to them. As one of her favorite human aphorisms held, you must be present to win. Showtime.

Gus attended to the instruments and controls as they skirted the pier, the hum of the electric motor nearly inaudible. Dugan scanned the steel pilings for anything irregular, and watched Spence and Pearl conduct closer inspection. He could now see the evenly spaced depressions in the sand, lining out of sight toward the shore, but nothing else of note. Gus commented that watching Pearl in the water was entirely pleasant, and that Spence obviously shared the feeling. Steadying his course along the pier, Gus spotted what looked like a cylindrical bathysphere sitting on end on the bottom. "What the hell is that gray thing?" he asked.

"That's Leona Philpot," Dugan replied. "It's a Microsoft experimental data center, using ocean water to cool the components. An external hard drive and data transmitter, and potential power generator. Cal Poly provided the hookup to the pier."

"Potentially powered by what?"

"Wave motion, prop-driven turbines off the coast at Vandenberg."

"And they call it Leona?"

"Guess it's the name of a company video game character."

"Cute," Gus said. Halfway along the pier he pointed at eight o'clock, "That divot over there is backwards."

Dugan leaned forward squinting. Sure enough, where the spacing would put a bowl was a slightly convex rise in the sand. The divers passed it unnoticed behind them, their attention on the pier. "Let's check that on the way back," he said, and radioed Jack to inform the divers. "It could be just tidal movement, but we gotta have a look."

He asked Gus if the panoramic video was being recorded. "'Tis, twice. We have a recorder on board and a transmitter sending it to one in the van. We could send it out live if we had a satellite link."

"That would be something, if there was anything to see. Another question, do you have lights in back as bright as the fronts?"

Gus admitted they were weaker LEDs, bit of an afterthought, and that that would be a useful improvement. Dugan didn't mention the source of his question, which was the uncertainty of having seen or not the random presence of shadowed globular objects in the aft camera monitors, and behind them larger, darker figures. He had the sense they were being followed, but was reluctant to alarm the pilot, and busied himself shifting his view between the divers and the video screens.

"We're getting into shallow water," Gus reported, "shall we swing south?"

"Yeah, let's follow the shoreline at this depth, out to the point at Pirate's Cove, then back across in deeper water and look at that hump." He radioed Jack and Hank to inform the divers and glanced again at the monitor. They were there alright, clearly the sinuous, luminescent outlines of jellyfish, and their numbers were legion. On the other hand, they appeared to be unarmed.

While Spence had always considered natural selection a sound theory, watching Pearl move through the water offered strong evidence for the notion of intelligent design. Even encased in the unnatural equipage of diving gear, her form and movement invoked the possibility of creative choice, a cosmic architect of elegance, an artistic master of sculptural beauty. Her radio cut the thought short.

"Spence, we're bearing right. Are you still with us?"

"Right behind you," he said happily.

Much as she loved diving for its own sake, Pearl was keen to meet her new maternal mentor, felt her presence nearby, and found herself humming the tune to "Magical Mystery Tour." Following which Spence came back with a few bars of "Octopus's Garden." Jack and Hank continued the Beatles theme with:

> Little darling, it's been a long cold lonely winter
> Little darling, it feels like years since it's been here
> Here comes the sun
> Here comes the sun, and I say
> It's all right

Monitoring the radios on shore, Gina and Gloria were nearly through side two of the "Abbey Road" album when Gus came back on the horn. "Okay, we're about to head back, just have to check out a bulge on this side of the pier. Give you a heads up when we make the turn."

"Ten-four," Gloria replied. She made no mention of the two suits in a Lincoln town car parked across the road, who seemed to be making a long meal out of a Cuban sandwich. Getting hungry, she had to have a look with the binoculars. She loved Cuban sandwiches.

"Everything jake up there?" he asked.

"Well…, there are a couple birddogs in a sensible sedan, been parked by the road for a half hour."

Gus asked for a description, to which Dugan replied. "No worries, those are the Mormon drug agents. They've been watching us for awhile, just don't act suspicious."

Which made Gina wonder what she might do if she didn't want to look suspicious, or what acting like you were not acting suspicious would look like. She could think of several actors who had no trouble at all looking questionable. She wondered if the two guys were NSA, watching her for any contact with Leon. She felt suspected, and more than a little pissed off.

"Maybe we should just put in on this side of the pier," Gus said. "I don't want to deal with any feds."

"No, that would just draw attention," replied Dugan. "We're just recreational boaters going back to the ramp."

Gus allowed as how they could stay under another forty minutes with no problem. Dugan had a closer look at the screens, now absent anything visible behind them. Up ahead Pearl was motioning down at the hummock she had missed before, and Gus moved the sub in for a closer look. Spence descended, took a few profile shots of the swell and noted the dimensions, then began scooping away sand at the top. Gus brought the sub to rest on the bottom, facing the pier, with lights and camera on the action as Pearl dove to assist with sweeping.

The submariners could now see a light silver-bronze domed shell, with only slight radius, emerge from the sand. As Pearl drew near, Spence suddenly ceased brushing, opened his arms and began floating to the surface as if caught in an invisible net. Her descent stopped in mid-stroke, as she was left suspended six feet from the crown. Her body would not respond to her brain's swimming signals. Pearl was about to report her situation when her radio popped and died, as did the power supply on Clamantine.

The available light at thirty feet gave Dugan and Gus a softly dimmed blue-green view of the scene, one they would scarce forget. And one they could document, since the only electrical power left on the sub derived from the back-up batteries for the video cameras. Gus had a look at Dugan, who showed some apprehension. "Okay, all systems but one are down," he said, "but we have oxygen if necessary. And if we do have to get out, we can swim to the surface from here."

"That's reassuring," Dugan replied. "Meanwhile we have the issue of whatever that is coming out of the sand, and what's happening to Pearl." He knew, more or less, what was coming into view before them, knowing as well that he couldn't inform Gus. The threat of danger was absent.

As Edna rose, the covering of sand slowly cascading down, Pearl came to rest on top, her arms spread in embrace, as a child would hug her mother. Gus reached for a knob and brought up the gain on the cameras. Better detail showed Pearl's eyes closed, the bubbles from her tanks signaling normal breathing. The resolution also brought the background into view, illuminating a company of jellyfish in formation, and behind them between the steel pilings of the pier, a platoon of tall frog-like creatures standing as sentinels. Both men were transfixed by the image. "This must be the main feature," said Dugan.

Jack and Hank were also dead in the water with no engine power or radios. Only the battery pack for Mark's video kit was operational, so he could still monitor activities below at a wide angle. At slack tide they were able to maintain position with oars. Spence made several attempts to go back down, but could only go a few feet until a steady wave of reverse-gravity energy stopped him. When the Zodiac pulled alongside he climbed aboard, where Hank was suiting up.

Pulling his mouthpiece Spence shouted, "Don't bother! You can only get..." but Hank was already over the side.

Thirty-Two

Pearl was nervous but unafraid. Before falling into a state of what she would come to call "pure consciousness," her heartbeat slowed, breathing deepened, and she was held suspended as Edna came up to meet her. There she settled atop the shell, arms and legs splayed, looking from Dugan's point of view like a large purple starfish.

Hank dove to within ten feet of Clamantine when his forward progress was stopped by some force. He could see Gus and Dugan, who turned to spot him. His palms-up signal brought an OK sign from Dugan, allowing him to literally and figuratively breathe easier. Gus emerged from a speechless trance of unknown length and said, "My goodness. That's really something." He observed that while the cameras were still working, the transmitter wasn't. And that the recorder may no longer have power.

"So we may be watching this performance for the first and last time," Dugan said. Though he felt rather than knew that this creature, whom he had just christened Edna the Great, likely had both the ability and foresight to provide a record of her premier appearance. And that if not she would probably make her second show available to a much wider audience.

As the minutes ticked by outside the pierside bubble of slow-motion animation, Gloria and Gina worried at the radio silence, but not suspiciously. Through the pilings they caught glimpses of the boats, which were holding position. "They may just be busy," Gloria observed. "But if it goes much longer I'll suit up and go have a look." Then she remembered the satellite phone in the glovebox, and that Jack had one on the boat. But when she turned it on there was no signal. Worrisome, although she still had line of sight on her man.

"I have a kayak on my truck," Gina said. "We can both go across under the pier."

"That would look suspicious, and we wouldn't want to leave our gear untended with the gourmet voyeurs still on duty." They agreed to watch and wait. Gloria glanced at the twosome in the Lincoln, who now appeared to be eating fish tacos.

...

Although Pearl had never considered herself a good classroom student, the current symposium had her total attention. She felt as if an old friend was leading her by baby steps through an immense compendium of historical events and people, compiled and smoothly edited in a timeline of radio broadcasts, newspaper clips and television reports. She was presented an infinite buffet of social, political and scientific data, in small portions. Academic arcana was distilled into digestible nuggets, economic and military machinations outlined in simple terms, corporate manipulations of elected officials and public policy, galloping incompetence among security agencies, punctuated by drunken celebrations of stupidity...

The enormity of mankind's systematic and inexorable destruction of the planet's basic ecosystems was staggering, presented to her by example in plain language and vivid illustration. Edna had chosen to approximate the human voice that Pearl would find most comfortable, the soothing tones of the poet Maya Angelou. She encouraged her student to focus her future research on the causes of what she called "the obdurate persistence of ignorance." What could possibly account, she asked, for the exponential march of humans to poison themselves?

Pearl began to feel more like a great-granddaughter in this equation, that generations of experience with trial and error brought an unequivocal wisdom to the narrative, that it was trustworthy. Stories of people "who knew their business," as Granny would say, and profiles of those who didn't, but could convince their followers otherwise. The art of the con. "Same old story," Grampy always said.

Snookered, scammed, bamboozled, ripped off. Time and again, one generation to the next. Go figure.

Edna's other question for Pearl concerned gender, the hanging unanswered question in her extensive scholarship. How was it that the humans were among the few species with such widespread fear of the female? She knew the popular fable of the primal man and woman in the garden, with a snake selling apples. Was it merely a grim parable that centuries of repetition had given the stamp of fact? She was left with the wandering tides of speculation.

Perhaps the phobia derived from some ancient mix-up of algorithms, which produced an arcane cryptography by a pre-human lifeform, in a primordial swamp on the dark side of the moon. She hoped it wasn't just a joke by the mistress of the universe. Pearl had to admit she might be of little help with this line of inquiry. While the drift into destruction of the habitat was an almost exclusively male enterprise, it was also clear they wouldn't likely be persuaded to turn it around any time soon.

"That's why we've come to meet this way, dear," Edna said softly. "To get their attention."

• • •

"Unless you want to backtrack," Gus said, "we can cut across under the pier, still water and plenty of clearance."

"Good by me," said Dugan. "Startin' to feel a little claustrophobic anyway, nothin' personal."

As they passed over Edna's spot, now returned to concave shape, he scanned the middle screens. The pier's steel pilings were encrusted with barnacles, sea urchins and clumps of unrecycled metal and plastic detritus from the human visitors. Visibility had dropped in the late-morning shadow of the pier, but not enough to obscure the object attached to the last piling to port. An image the mariners would later concur might have been best left unseen. And unrecorded.

"That appears to be a human form embracing that post," Gus noted. As they moved in the camera showed what remained of a middle-aged man's face, missing the nose, eyeballs and an ear. Wearing only a leather jacket, his hands and feet were bound with plastic bags. Even without the facial features, what was left indicated his final expression was one of surprise.

Gus put the sub on the bottom. "He also has a tail fin." Dugan squinted to make out the appendage, and noted the familiar round magazine pressed against the man's buttocks.

"No, that there is the back half of a Tommy Gun."

"An actual Chicago Typewriter?"

"Very same," Dugan replied. He didn't mention having seen the gun before, but allowed as how they had just found what appeared to be the missing fisherman, whom he would refer to hereafter as Marty Thompson. Reference to the final resting place of the machine gun would usually be omitted in polite conversation.

The rest of the crew was waiting at the ramp. Jack and Simon stood waist-deep to steady the sub while Dugan and Gus climbed out. They were loaded and on the road within minutes, headed for Wooly's and a Cuban sandwich, at Gloria's suggestion. The hungry Mormons fell in behind.

• • •

The crew reassembled on the deck at Wooly's over sandwiches, tacos, nachos and a Leinenkugel Grapefruit Shandy. Hunger overtook conversation, until Pearl took a deep breath and said, "Oh, God, I can't begin to tell you guys what I learned from Edna. Literally, I can't, because this is the first order for now. We have to be ready to go tomorrow morning. Both boats, out at the weather buoy, and she'll give us a signal. I think she just wants friendly witnesses, and… well, maybe some protection. She'll only have so much time, and she doesn't want anyone to get hurt. But she wants to make a statement."

Seven faces regarded her with combined bewilderment and understanding. This was it, the big do-dah day. What ever have we gotten ourselves into, and hey let's go find out. They had already accepted the mission.

"Uh, I have a question," Spence said. "What exactly do you mean by protection? From, like, the city police or the Coast Guard? The Air Force?"

"Vandenberg can have PT boats and choppers here in less than fifteen minutes" Jack observed. "F-16s in about half that. Will they shoot if civilians are in the target zone? No way to know. That always comes down to the guy in charge."

He caught Dugan's slight smile. Normally they would fall into the dialogue between General Jack D. Ripper and Group Captain Lionel Mandrake in the film "Doctor Strangelove." But this was the real combination plate, no disco foolin' around. Automatic weapons can be dangerous in the wrong hands. Perhaps there is a reasonable limit on the extent to which one must go to protect an endangered species. But what if we are one of them?

"According to my information," Pearl said, "the, uh, demonstration will last less than five minutes. We only have to stand by, windward of the big swells, and then escort Edna out of the bay."

"What big swells?" Hank asked.

"I assume she's bringing them," replied Pearl.

Thirty-Three

Dugan was afoot before sunrise the next day, the traditional October Pismo Beach Clam festival, with the inkling that this edition would become most memorable. The beachfront booths were assembling, soon to offer up games of chance, clam chowder, souvenirs, burritos, churros and salt water taffy. The marching bands had yet to convene or pose for photos in their traditional Cowboy, Portuguese, Swiss or Mexican outfits; the local rock, reggae and Tex-Mex bands were sleeping off last night's gig. But the town was set to party.

Dugan had decided to forego notifying the local authorities of the armed man under the pier, choosing to wait until after the festivities. Officer Mike, aka Captain Sweeny, was busy at his desk checking assignments for the additional law enforcement dictated by the festival. Always a pain in the ass, but rarely cause for concern beyond the few drunks that had to go in the tank overnight, a couple scuffles between the college students and local aggies, surfers and biker clubs. He had always taken the minimalist approach to crowd control, having learned in Chicago that aggressive restrictions usually created more problems than they solved. His father, a beat cop there in '68, never tired of blaming the "communist hippie scum" for the violence at the Democratic convention.

Now, with another emotional and divisive presidential election campaign in its final weeks, and the added element of jihadist and domestic terrorism in the blender, Mike recalled another of his dad's favorite sentiments, "You can never be too careful." But given the results of the war On Drugs and the one On Terror, Mike had come to take exception to the traditional admonition. Seems that sometimes you can be too careful. Albeit there were times when, no matter how much care has been taken, we are quite unprepared for what may be appearing around the bend.

It appeared simultaneously to Dugan and Mike, to the first visually, the second by phone. Dugan spoke the words to himself, with some incredulity, while scanning the south shore with binoculars; Sweeny heard them distinctly from Deputy Stowell in Oceano, but still asked that he repeat them. "What do you mean...?"

"THE DUNES ARE GONE!"

Both parties to the news took pause to consider it, and checked their sources again for confirmation, Dugan by adjusting the focus on his binoculars. Sweeny gathered his thoughts, called the dispatcher to notify the Harbor Patrol, Sheriff and Search and Rescue. "Cordon off the entrance and exit," he told Stowell. "I'll be there in five minutes." In the car he radioed State Parks, Highway Patrol and surrounding city police departments, signaling the possible need for traffic control. When asked why, he told them that the dunes were gone. "What do you mean...?"

Dugan went to the deck and the big telescope; indeed the southern reach of the Pismo beach was flat, looking quite like a pristine sweep of white sand stretching from Arroyo Grande creek to Point Sal. The shoreline looked as if the Pismo Dunes State Preserve and Vehicular Recreation Area had never existed. Quite a diversionary tactic he thought when the phone rang. "Time to go," Pearl said. Game on.

. . .

He filled a thermos with coffee and headed to the garage. Jack was already putting fresh tanks and gear bags in the back of Dugan's old Chevy Suburban, as Gloria filled a basket with avocados, trail mix, fruit and cheese. Dugan grabbed two bottles of Adelaide pinot noir. Who knew how long they'd be on the water. A picnic adventure!

Hank steadied the Zodiac as Pearl and Mark loaded their gear, Spence and Gina were ready at the panga, where Hank had been instructed to put his longboard. Jenny had accepted her assignment to stay ashore and observe for the record. Byrnes, Jack and Gloria arrived to the accompaniment of sirens from the south, a helicopter approaching from the east, and a drone that swept by overhead. Quickly they were on the water.

Pearl's seminar with Edna had ended without drama. Her student status was over and now some excitement was on the way, and she rather enjoyed the role of… production assistant? But Hank made claim to the title, saying she was obviously the assistant director. "I'll make this thing go where you want," he said. "You're the chosen one, my dear. It's up to you to make sure no gets hurt, right? Including us."

Few among the gathering festival crowd noticed the absence of police in Pismo Beach. The lights and sirens of police cars headed into Oceano continued, and a CHP chopper came over fast and low from the north. Some of the early crowd on the pier paused to watch Hank ripping across a five-foot wave breaking sixty yards out. A few noticed the unusual shift from a north to a south break, and back again. And that the surfer was covering some real distance, fast, then kicking out and coming back on the next set. Weird.

As the sirens diminished, the sounds made a seamless segue into what one listener later compared to the synthesizer in the tune "Oh, What a Lucky Man" by Emerson, Lake and Palmer. The chords and soaring notes swept back and forth in the wind, passing over the pier in sonic waves. "The effect was hypnotic," another recalled later, unaware that everyone there had in fact been hypnotized. Their heads swiveled in unison, watching Hank go back and forth, as if they were viewing a slow-motion tennis match.

Jack brought the panga alongside at the terminus on the leeward side, with Pearl and Gina in the Zodiac positioned on the other. Gloria and Gina each held a bullhorn, as Hank surfed in and boarded the panga, and the music faded. Mark wondered where the audio was coming from.

Alternating, the women hailed the spectators above. "HELLO on the pier! We have received a Coast Guard alert! High wave activity may make the pier dangerous. They're asking everyone to move slowly off the pier." Mark zoomed in on the faces forty feet above, some people leaning out, cupping theirs ears. The surf was now audible. Most of the people waved and nodded as the boats came slowly past, and began walking. By the time the boats were nearly at the beach, the waves at the outer end of the pier were breaking at twenty feet.

Then the pier began to shake gently, as if swaying slightly in a high wind. At which a few people started running and others picked up their pace. As the oscillation's frequency rose, everyone was running, the Rod & Boogie Board Rental stand began dancing on its fitments, awning boards flapping, snacks and fishing gear spouting onto the pier. Diners on the deck at Wooly's looked up at the sound of screaming.

Thirty-Four

Edna had planned her appearance with care. Removing the dunes at night had required some study of their composition, the tide tables and a review of fluid dynamics, but was fairly easy to accomplish. She thought the new sand bar looked quite nice. The motorized recreation fans would lament the loss of a playground, but higher priorities had come into play.

At sunrise she generated repeating signals to effectively jam all radio and phone communications in a 30-mile radius, including satellite transmissions. Unless the feds had eyes on from above, Vandenberg would be out of the loop for awhile. Local television media wouldn't arrive in time to broadcast the day's events live, so it would be up to Mark and the thousands of cell phones on shore to record her presentation. Hank was happy to perform the pre-game show on his surfboard. Radio communication between her friends and guardians would remain active on a secure frequency.

At flood tide she began a series of long swooping figure-eights, tracing barrel rolls on each eastern loop, slowly building the bi-directional incoming swell. Moving toward shore, she could see Hank's board slicing by above and gaining speed. When the pier began to sway, Edna delivered her surfing pal to Jack's boat and switched to an oval pattern, banking sharply on the inland radius, magnifying the waves now breaking due east on the beach.

The pier had emptied by the time she reached shallow water, the parking lot was evacuating quickly, and diners in the second floor oyster bar at Wooly's looked down to see waves lapping through the upper deck. Customers and staff were half-swimming out of Pancho's Surf Shop, the Arcade, Splash Cafe and Cool Cat. The edge of panic was at hand. This could be the big one.

At that point, as Henry would always remember and proudly

tell the next generation of patrons at the bar, the news was delivered to Harry's by none other than Herb Tuttle, man of few words, who burst into the bar and yelled, "IT'SAGIANTFUCKINGCLAM!"

Within two minutes the water was bubbling up through the pool table pockets in the old theater on Pomeroy, and the intersection at Price Street, clogged with traffic, was approaching knee deep. The swell stopped short of the highway, but southbound motorists had stopped to watch the bedlam below, blocking Highway 101 from Squire Canyon to Arroyo Grande. The north and southbound entrance ramps were likewise jammed, effectively blocking exit and entry to Pismo Beach. Edna had the attention of thousands.

Nonetheless, as she knew, some residents of the surrounding condos and hillside palaces were resolute defenders of the public safety and national interest. Retired military, law enforcement and self-appointed militia who would already be on the move, certain that they had just seen a flying saucer manned by aliens or commies at the beach. Edna was unconcerned with drones, even armed, since she could alter their flight path at will. What kind of firepower might arrive by vehicle or on foot was another matter. Her shell could deflect rounds of significant caliber and velocity, but the surrounding humans stood at real risk. Collateral injures would diminish the impact of her message.

As she eased out of the wave generation whirlpool the water level began subsiding, leaving a block-square pool in the new hotel excavation site next to the Cool Cat Cafe. Spectators on top of the hotel were pointing at what appeared to be several frogmen in the water, rigging a speaker to the exposed arm of a submerged backhoe. Then their attention went to the bay, and what some took for the top of a remote-control submarine, until the dolphins arrived.

Edna's propulsion system simulated a jet ski, the intake and expulsion of water powered by her own electric motor. At full power she could clear the water by thirty feet, and remain airborne for five seconds. As the break receded from shore she caught a wave that closed out half-way down the pier, hit the throttle and cleared the railings by eight feet, skipping three times across the surf parallel to shore and came about. The crowd roared.

The dolphins arrived on cue, lifted her to nearly above the water and sped toward the former dunes where Officer Mike stood with a pair of binoculars and a cruiser that wouldn't start. Some two dozen police, fire and emergency crews found themselves stranded on the new beach at Oceano, without running vehicles or communicators. Stymied.

Some spectators returned to the beach with the ebbing surf, feeling the threat of danger had evaporated. A few looked around for film crews, thinking they might be taking part in a movie shoot or TV commercial. The flying clam could be some kind of Hollywood special effects technology, animatronics or maybe a hologram. Then, as the speeding ensemble arced out to sea and came around toward shore, the dolphins leapt in synchronized grace, their passenger briefly airborne, her escorts diving and reappearing before the shell touched the water. As Edna approached the beach at speed, the crowd could clearly make out her size.

"What is that, Dad?" asked one youngster. "I'm not sure, son, but it looks like a very very large clam."

Jack and Pearl kept their boats on the perimeter, keeping alternating eyes on the shoreline and the sky as Mark followed Edna with his camera. No sign of aircraft so far, though a drone had appeared from the south at a hundred feet, but changed direction erratically as it approached, wobbled, did a couple loops then shot upwards and out of sight. Dugan replaced his carbine in the scabbard attached to his seat.

Then they heard the sound of dirt bikes. Hank and Gina turned their binoculars toward Shell Beach as Edna slowed, released the dolphins and submerged. Looking through the pier they saw two dual-sport bikes followed by a black Hummer H2 with shiny oversized wheels. Both bikes carried a rider and passenger, all in camouflage gear and carrying AR15s. All were moving quickly.

Edna gave Jack and Hank their options for positions, considering the possible line of fire, and Jack quickly swung the panga to put them between her and the beach. Edna added that she hoped to disarm the troops quickly, since the timepiece was ticking and she still had an essential meeting with the spectators.

The riders passed under the pier, their passengers at port arms and scanning the bay. Pearl waved from the Zodiac without response. They showed more interest In Jack's boat, nearer shore, as the lead passenger put his glasses on it and the trailing bike's tailgunner stood on the pegs with his rifle ready. The crowd had backed up into the parking lot when the Hummer reached the apex of the shoreline, where the back doors opened and two men emerged with automatic weapons and stood on the running boards.

At Edna's signal, Jack slammed the throttle and the panga was out of range before anyone on hand could say Danger, Will Robinson! Which owed largely to Edna's sudden rise from the water about ninety feet offshore, sending a fast, shallow wave to the beach. The Hummer turned sharply to the sea and the two rear passengers opened fire. The bikes were turning around when the wave from Edna's exit reached their wheels. One rider noticed, just before his faceshield hit the sand, that the water seemed to be full of jellyfish.

Hank wicked up the Zodiac at the sound of gunfire and headed for the pier. As he cut back toward the beach, Pearl put the glasses on the gunmen. Edna had moved closer to shore, showing no apparent damage from the bullets, as the wave moved back to the sea, carrying with it the Hummer. Apparently assisted by the jellyfish. All the occupants bailed out before the vehicle submerged, and scrambled after their motorcycle escorts, who were on foot, and kept slipping, falling and screaming with stinging pain. The crowd cheered wildly.

• • •

Henry had shut down the power in the bar when the water began rising, dumped the cash drawer in a bag, grabbed a bottle of Jameson Black Barrel and headed for the roof of the hotel. Jenny was stationed at the corner with a cassette tape recorder, camera and a walkie-talkie. Two dozen hotel guests crowded the edge.

"Haven't seen one of those for years," he said. "Old school."

"She said this was the only way we could keep in touch."

"She?"

"Edna."

"Right," Henry said, wondering what she may have been smoking, and did she have any more. "Who's Edna?"

"She's right there!" Jenny pointed at the shore, where he turned to see what was indeed, by all appearances, a giant fucking clam. And a black Hummer sliding into the surf as four armed passengers exited in haste, and what actually looked like teams of jellyfish carrying their weapons and two dirt bikes out to sea. Henry took two glasses from the bag and poured each with three fingers of whiskey. Setting one in front of Jenny, he raised the other. "Here's to Edna."

Mark's wife, whose name no one could ever remember, appeared behind them. "Henry! Is Mark out there getting shot at?!" He admitted not knowing, but that Jenny may have more current information, and that she was pretty busy at the moment. His attention returned to the beach when Jenny's walkie-talkie squawked. "Yes, okay… Roger that… Gotcha, ten-four!"

Henry awaited new information while she quickly gathered her gear. "We've got to get people off the roof," she said. "Edna says the alarm went off at Vandenberg, and they're scrambling pilots now. We may all be in the middle of a battle zone in a few minutes."

193

Using his outdoor voice, Henry stood on a milk crate and addressed the crowd. "LADIES and gentleman! We've just been informed of a possible… national defense situation. This has been designated a restricted area! For your own safety, please return to your rooms!" Peering over the edge, he could see the water on the street was only ankle deep and draining back to shore. As he and Jenny funneled people to the stairs, she turned to see the top of the Hummer disappear under water, and Edna slide onto the beach next to the pier.

Thirty-Five

Edna had given her public address debut a cursory rehearsal, and was now aware that it would have to be succinct. While her thick armor plating could easily withstand small arms fire, rockets and guided missiles were another kettle of fish, another human term she found puzzling.

Jenny hit the street running as the crowd, showing no fear, flowed onto the beach and began surrounding the glistening shell. She made it to the lifeguard tower and retrieved the camera and recorder from her backpack, looking up to see Jack and Pearl ease their boats to the waterline. Looking back she could see two men in suits on the hotel roof, both holding binoculars. The platform put her just above the perimeter of a human circle, six deep, surrounding a huge clam, at high tide. The story was taking shape. Who knew?

She checked her equipment batteries, paused to wonder what had become of Henry, and heard Mark clattering up the steps carrying three video cameras and a tripod. Jenny waved at the boaters and exchanged thumbs-ups, as the Pismo Eight collectively pondered just what this finale might involve. And what their guard duties would require, and, come success or failure, what would be next? Perhaps Edna would let them know.

Jack and Hank kept eyes to the southwest, from whence the military aircraft would likely approach, while Gloria and Pearl attended the ridgeline behind the highway, the path of best disguise for pilots. That the fighters would be well-armed was a given, whether or not Edna could mess with their guidance systems remained an open question. Everyone knew the answer was on the way.

Dugan held the least apprehension, maybe just a function of seniority. His concern went to those in the Zodiac, who were most vulnerable, but knew they were capable young folks. If they could just get the mothership out to sea, the rest would take care of itself. He would have stories for his grandchildren, assuming they would inherit a habitable planet, and the satisfaction of having played a role in the drama that helped ensure they got one. The hopey-changey stuff.

Edna now had a captive audience, if only for the next few minutes. Those in the motorist balcony on the highway strained to see what was going on below, the parking lot was jammed, half the pier had filled again, and all those assembled wondering if they could, in fact, believe their eyes. And the surrounding ring of a few hundred humans, with whom she would have direct contact, holding hands and becoming, she hoped, a powerful enclosure of collective consciousness. Or, at least, awareness.

Since the outlying crowd was beyond the circle of influenced, she would have to keep their attention with music. Her frog-men had installed four large speakers, she had Dugan's music library at hand, and selected a medley she hoped would hold the audience and play them out on her departure. She chose "Nights in White Satin" by the Moody Blues, and Procul Harum's "Whiter Shade of Pale." The inner circle, occupying their own sound chamber in which only they could hear, would share another song.

First she radiated a warm glow to relax the large circle of friends, asking them to hold hands and greet their neighbors. She suggested they think of the gathering as a campfire chat, even though the communication would be one way, that later they would employ to generate useful dialogue with others. She had listened to several Ted Talks.

Her presentation simulated the sermon she had given Pearl. But with hundreds of receptors, she could parcel the information into more and smaller packets, with distribution made unto every man according "as he had need," as she had read in a book called the "New Testament." The addendum – from each according to his ability – arrived later with French socialism in the 19th century, she learned, then adopted by Russians who attempted to base a society on it. Edna realized it was unlikely that she would ever come to know what her message produced from the humans' abilities, their best or otherwise.

She began with a simple tour of the local waters, the recent abrupt changes in its temperature and chemistry, and the results among fish, mammals and the human economy. The show, enhanced by holograms, included graphics of some disturbing mutations in the ocean, and a few from the recent political campaign among humans on land. Several mothers instinctively covered their children's eyes, although the images were internal for all. The crowd was attentive.

"My name is Edna," she said. "I'm here to help." Her exhibition focused on two themes: First, choose your friends wisely (at which she felt having set a good example), and Second, we don't have much time. To illustrate the first point, she provided a detailed list of public officials, military leaders and business executives who, in the past seventy-five years, had not acted as their friends. And what the costs had been, in livelihoods and lives. Bills they had paid, and were still paying. Why and how they could withhold payment. And, for those with sufficient internal hard drives, a complete bibliography of reliable documentation on both friendship and time. The point on Time, which included a three-dimensional display of the food chain collapsing, was interrupted by a signal from Pearl.

Absorbed in her tutorial, she had allowed her own jamming system to falter, as a Viper attack helicopter slipped over the ridge and landed on the hotel roof. Edna put her classroom on hold and attended to her transmitter and frequencies, and got back to her favorite observer in the Zodiac. Pearl reported two men in suits approaching the pilots, talking and pointing at the beach. As they moved away the noise of the chopper's engine rose, but the rotor gained no speed. At more throttle the sound came up briefly, followed by a sudden billow of blue smoke when the blades stopped. A temporary fix.

Time. Too little remained to both complete the lesson and test her defenses against the jets that would soon arrive. So she delivered a capsule synopsis of the critical food curriculum, with a list of key references to check on Google, and the address for a YouTube video displaying the most credible timeline for environmental and economic failure, and tips to avoid its eventuality.

"But our time together here is brief," she said. "In the small amount we have left, let us sing." She had chosen her friends' favorite band.

When I find myself in times of trouble, Mother Mary comes to me
Speaking words of wisdom, let it be
And in my hour of darkness she is standing right in front of me
Speaking words of wisdom, let it be
Let it be, let it be, let it be, let it be
Whisper words of wisdom, let it be
And when the broken hearted people living in the world agree
There will be an answer, let it be
For though they may be parted, there is still a chance that they will see
There will be an answer, let it be
Let it be, let it be, let it be, let it be

The F-16 Falcons arrived in two pairs, from the southwest and east, the first at 200 feet over the water, the other two at a thousand feet. Their trajectories intersected above the pier, the lower duo peeling off to north and south as their teammates continued out to sea and came around together. While the roar of their engines had the inland crowd cowering, it went unheard by the unbroken circle of singers. The choir then parted slowly to seaward, still holding hands and singing, as Edna slid into the water. She tuned in to the pilots' radio channel as Pearl and Jack came alongside and she put the aircraft on the intercom.

"Brutus this is Team Hunter over Pismo, come back."

"Roger, Hunter. Colonel Proctor here. What do you see?"

"Coming around for a better look, but the town and freeway are jammed with people, and there's a large circle of people on the beach. They're surrounding a large sort of round object, and it looked like they were singing. We're coming in for a better look."

"That object look like a flying saucer?"

"No sir, that wouldn't be my first guess."

"What did it look like?"

"A giant clam, sir."

Thirty-Six

The crews in both boats shared a good laugh at the pilot's reply, but everyone felt the bittersweet twinge of the moment. They knew this was it, Edna's farewell. The jets were headed back at reduced speed, but she was now submerged as the two boats closed above her. Two planes were only a hundred feet off the water when they crossed overhead, the pilots' faces visible as they banked. Jenny and Mark, who had sprinted from the beach to Jack's boat just in time, trained their cameras on the aircraft.

"Team Hunter here. The object on the beach is no longer visible and the crowd is breaking up. Traffic on the freeway is underway. Looks like the Viper on top of the hotel is disabled, we have no radio contact. Awaiting instructions, out."

"What about the spot where the object was before?"

"It looks like a sand trap divot from an enormous wedge."

"Roger that. Anything else worth checking out?"

"There are two boats headed out of the bay side by side, a panga and a Zodiac, four civilians aboard each. No weapons visible. Looks like they're having a party. Nothing suspicious, but the guy at the wheel is wearing some kind of Indian head dress and war paint on his face."

"That's it?"

"Well, he just looked up and gave me the finger."

"I'll be damned," said the colonel. "Sounds like this was some kind of hoax or publicity stunt to get our attention. You guys are clear to return to base."

"Roger, I'll make another low pass for pictures and head home. Hunter out."

Edna's regatta was a half-mile offshore when the pilot came around and brought his plane in fifty feet off the water, almost at stall speed. At 200 yards, approaching the boats his engine flamed out, but airspeed speed dropped only slightly, then slowed more with no loss of altitude. Just above the boats, the F-16 stopped, rotated 180 degrees and hung there suspended.

Gloria squinted to make out his identification, upside down, now above the cockpit. The pilot regarded the crew members with some surprise. An old guy at the back of the panga raised a glass of red wine and gave him a salute, a man and woman in the middle were taking pictures of him, and in the Zodiac a beautiful young woman in purple smiled and waved. He had no instrument readings or radio, he thought, until a voice came on.

"Do I have the pleasure of addressing Captain Thomas P. Albion of the U.S. Air Force?" The voice quality registered somewhere between Morgan Freeman and Jack Nicholson. "You do," the pilot replied. "May I ask your name, and what you've done to my plane?"

"You can call me Ed," came the reply. "Control of your vehicle will be returned shortly. First you should know that the people in the boats are leaving now, and that the photos you've taken of them have been erased. Unlike theirs of you. Then I'll give you a brief orientation and you'll be home in time for dinner."

"Looks like you're in charge, Ed."

Headed for shore at a leisurely pace, the crews listened to Edna's lecture to the pilot. She traced, in broad terms, his country's history of national warfare from 1898 to the present, the policy rationale for each conflict, who initiated them, paid the costs, who profited, and those who died. In the few cases his country could call victories, she itemized the long-term results over the past 70 years; draining the national resources, dividing the population into opposing factions, poisoning the land, air and water, and destabilizing other countries around the world. Apparently with the primary purpose of maintaining its position as the planet's foremost maker and seller of military weapons.

As a footnote, Edna cited the continuing confusion among humans regarding the motivation for killing, among groups or individuals. Her research had revealed only two, greed or revenge. Either the killers wanted something the others had, or sought to retrieve something the others had taken. And that both motives predated by centuries any forms of organized political, religious or social constructs. She noted the popular definition of insanity as trying the same thing over and over, hoping for a different result.

"I certainly make no claim as a psychiatrist," she said. "But it definitely sounds like one good way to define stupidity. So there you have it, captain, food for thought as your species say. And may I add, as a parting note, that according to all the evidence available, which is all the evidence, your people haven't lived in a representative democracy, or a constitutional republic, since 1948. Although the labels are still freely employed."

"I was born in 1984."

"Indeed, and now that your people are facing catastrophe, some of them want to elect a blabbering lout as their leader. Keep that in mind when you return to Airstrip One. There's work to be done, captain. You have to decide what will be your part of the job. Your plane will resume normal functions in a few seconds. Have a nice day."

"Over and out, Ed."

Jenny and Hank watched through binoculars as the jet rotated slowly to its previous axis, the engine fired, came up to speed and the plane departed the freeze-frame as if it had taken off from a carrier deck and turned south. "Damnd'est thing I ever saw," Hank said.

A calm sea let Mark keep the scene framed on his video camera, with a signal to a monitor clipped to the back of the forward port chair. "Check it out you guys, I think she's coming up to say goodbye."

Jack and Hank held the Zodiac against the side as Mark zoomed out a bit to frame the shot. A surface swell bubbled and subsided, then

Edna breached at vertical, shot to about thirty feet, spun, executed a graceful back flip and dove in. The video screen had the attention of all when she appeared again at surfing speed, headed for the boats and accelerating. At fifty yards Edna lifted to about sixty degrees, her vestigial tail fin skipping across the water, circled the boats and headed out to sea. One last leap, a barrel roll, and she slipped into the ocean.

"Man!" exclaimed Hank. "She did a freakin' wheelie!"

Thirty-seven

Pismo Beach the next day hosted two U.S. Navy destroyers, three Coast Guard cutters, a Chinook helicopter on the pier, a company of National Guard troops, and a quarter-mile of restricted beach area with armed soldiers on both sides of the pier. Someone mentioned a submarine. Military police patrolled the streets. The governor was due shortly, when he got off the phone with the president. With the national election just weeks away, this situation could get out of hand. A coast away, the secretaries of state and defense were packing suitcases, as were a dozen secret service agents.

Pomeroy Avenue below Cypress was blocked off, occupied by a half-dozen Jeeps, armored personnel carriers, Humvees and troops in desert fatigues. The media was kept a block from the beach. No one had yet tried to slip in a camera drone. Four military snipers were positioned at the corners of the hotel roof.

Henry approached the two young infantrymen in uniform at the bar. "You guys must be off duty."

"Right," said one. "Some kind'a fuckin' duty this is." Texas accent.

"Yeah," the other griped. "First it's some bullshit rumor about a flying saucer, then a giant clam. What the hell, man." Western Pennsylvania.

"I guess you haven't had a chance to check the Internet," Henry said.

"Nah, we were sittin' in a C-130 half the night, and the phones were blacked out. They don't let us know shit."

Henry punched up a Vimeo video on his phone, with some of Mark's footage, and handed it to the lads. "Let me buy you guys a beer," he said. "I think you're going to need it."

...

The Pismo Eight convened again on the deck at Dugan's bungalow that afternoon. A keg of Founders Harvest Ale nestled in an iced wine barrel bucket, the potluck spread featuring Jack's own guacamole, tri-tip Caesar salad, Korean spiced chicken wings, a pot of Gloria's clam chowder and a plate of San Luis Sourdough garlic bread. The vibe was festive.

"I think we can assume," the host proclaimed, "that if we haven't been investigated yet, we haven't been identified as suspects."

"Seems to me the only possible glitch could come from Captain Tom," Jenny said. "He of the upside-down fighter jet."

"This is just a theory," Mark said, "but I think she may have neuralyzed him."

"Say what?" Spence inquired.

"Remember that movie, 'Men in Black'? They had a neuralyzer, a flash that erased the memory of the suspects. When I had a tight shot, just before the plane rolled back over, I saw a flash reflect off the cockpit shell."

"That was a great movie," Hank said.

"You may be right," Jack offered. "But we were visible to everyone on the beach, and Sweeny had glasses on us from the dunes. Former dunes. Bet we'll be getting some questions soon enough."

At which they heard the sound of a motorcycle out front, followed by a knock at the door. "Harley Sportster," said Jack.

Dugan opened the door to find the same helmeted messenger who'd delivered Leon's first missive to Gina. "Is Mrs. Brennan here?"

"She is. Would you like to come in for some food? Maybe a barley sandwich?"

"Thanks, some other time," he said, offering another thumb drive. "Would you give her this please."

"Sure thing." He watched the mystery rider roll away, waiting to see if he'd been followed. He pocketed the drive, thinking it may best be delivered in the absence of company, and returned to the deck.

"Who was that?" Jack asked.

"Just a motorcycle buddy, thought I might want to go for a ride." He glanced at Gina. She knew. The day wound down as the assembly dined and drank, sharing their perceptions of the extraordinary events they'd seen, questioning their meaning and wondering what may lie ahead. They toasted Dugan for his coordination and leadership, and Pearl for her boldness and direct interaction with Edna. Implicit was the question of what she had learned.

"Thank you all," she said. "But she was the one in control. I think she has become my life instructor, my guru, that I've been awarded an honorary doctorate in oceanography. With emphasis on environmental science and climate change. Obviously we all now have a far higher awareness of the problems, and some sense of what we each can do to address them. So, as the public excitement subsides, which it soon will with the end of the presidential election carnival, we can meet for some real planning."

"Assuming we don't have a psychotic mutant in the White House," said Gloria.

"Do you think she'll come back?" Spence asked.

"I don't know," Pearl said. "She did grow up here, after all, but I think she felt her work in these waters was done. And that the coast will now be under constant surveillance. She did mention her concerns about the dead zone in the Gulf of Mexico, and that she wanted to look into the American and Russian saber-rattling in the Baltic Sea. Some pilots and ship captains may be in for a few surprises. Oh yeah, she also wants to head south and look into the degradation of the Great Barrier Reef."

"Maybe we'll run into her down there," Hank interjected.

"What do you mean?" asked Pearl.

"I have an offer on the shack. We could be in Australia for Christmas."

"Wow, who's the buyer?

"Henry. Much as he loves Harry's, said he was ready to spend more time on the beach and surfing. Think he's gotten a little weary of dealing with drunks."

Expressions of surprise made the rounds, all finding it hard to imagine their favorite bar without the world's best bartender. "Life moves on," said Gina. "Dugan, you have something for me?"

"Uhh… yeah, but thought it could wait till later."

"Now is good for me. We're all in this together."

Since some of the group knew only the outlines of Leon's situation, Dugan provided a brief summary and handed Gina the device. "You want to run it now?" She nodded, thinking whether it's for good or ill, the message would best be shared. Jenny produced her laptop, plugged in the drive and selected it. It was Leon's voice.

"Hi Mom. Just wanted you to know that Page and I are out of country, but not far away, safe and sound. No worries, but we won't be able to come back for awhile. Maybe if things shake out in a few months, you can come visit. Can't tell you about the place, but think you'll like it.

"Anyway, this deal started with the so-called Citizens United decision by the Supreme Court, the writing on the wall so to speak. We started talking about it with friends, off base, and thought about putting together a plan of action. Then came the WikiLeaks incident, the arrest of Bradley Manning, and the flight of Edward Snowden. We found ourselves living in a country we no longer recognized, could hardly believe what was happening. This is what I signed up to defend? Incredible.

Now we have the admission that the CIA was instrumental in the imprisonment of Nelson Mandela. Who are these people? How did they ever get put into positions of authority? What happened to our country?

"Long story short, somehow word got back to the base and I found myself facing the possibility of a court-martial. Then, with the advent of Trump and his league of vicious fearmongers, we decided it was time to split. Just didn't seem to be any way to work within the system. So a few friends and I are working from the outside, and we have some good tools, and access to most of the intelligence and military activities around the world. The current situation cannot stand. And if it does… well, we're thinking about Corsica. We can work from anywhere these days.

"I just hope this hasn't caused you too much grief, Mom. I hear you have a good friend in this Byrnes fellow, and that he's a good one to have on your side. More later. I love you."

Gina looked relieved. "Sounds like a good kid," Jack said. "Whatever happens down the road, he'll be on the right side of history." Jenny suggested he be made an honorary member of the team, in absentia, and agreement was unanimous.

Thirty-Eight

Edna, who had slipped back in with morning tide, monitored the gathering from just below the deck. Admittedly eavesdropping, but she didn't want to be a distraction, just to check on the welfare of her gang. Of whom she was quite proud. She couldn't imagine a better bunch of humans to have as friends.

Despite having her departure at hand, and the uncertain future, she was pleased. The years of loneliness were now as nothing, she would no longer wander as a solitary clam, but enjoy the communal bonds of the frog-men and the lovely jellies, and who knows what other species she might befriend. Cool, as the landers said.

She would surely find friendly waters, inhabited perhaps by life forms she had yet to encounter. Some who may also be mutations, who might share her conviction that some form of contentment was still possible in the ocean the landers called, without irony, the Pacific. And she was gratified to have brought more attention to their dangerous path of self-destruction. And that despite her unique condition, she would forever sail against the current, "borne back ceaselessly into the past." But at peace nonetheless, "happy as a clam at high tide."

As the sun touched the horizon, Edna selected her parting gift for the Pismo Eight, who she gathered subliminally to the railing. Their finest offering to her, which she would treasure beyond all else, was the music. Her library included everything from Pearl's computer, onshore radio stations, satellite music services and iPods on the beach. Sliding into the sea, she turned on Dugan's sound system and cued up a tune.

A couple hundred yards out, when the last liquid flare of sunlight leapt on the western rim, she hit the switch, having set the song to start just after the burst. The crew saw the green flash together, and had just time to gasp and holler in surprise, when the voice of Eva Cassidy came forth, and they embraced their partners and danced into the twilight.

> *You'll remember me when the west wind moves upon the fields of barley*
> *You'll forget the sun in his jealous sky as we walk in fields of gold*
> *So she took her love for to gaze awhile upon the fields of barley*
> *In his arms she fell as her hair came down among the fields of gold*
> *Will you stay with me, will you be my love among the fields of barley?*
> *We'll forget the sun in his jealous sky as we lie in fields of gold*
> *See the west wind move like a lover so upon the fields of barley*
> *Feel her body rise when you kiss her mouth among the fields of gold*

Epilogue

After the election, and its fearful result, the Pismo Eight became the Nine with the addition of young Mark as an official member. The prospect of the Apricot Apoplectic as commander in chief was now a reality, and each among them was sobered by the realization that history would record their efforts as a minor skirmish in the ongoing struggle against greed, bigotry and native ignorance. Sad.

"But they were not dismayed," wrote Jenny in her story for *Outside*. "Each of the Nine knew that the gift they had received from Edna would last a lifetime. That not even a federal coup by a cabal of feckless cretins would prevail in the face of truth, justice and the cosmic giggle." Byrnes got the last word. "The Pumpkin Bumpkin is the last chapter in the cartooning of America. If it's not a wake-up call, democracy has died. But it's been fun."

Dugan and Gina flirted with the notion of moving in together, but decided to let it simmer awhile. Pearl was transcribing her experience for either a doctoral thesis, a book or a National Geographic documentary. She hoped the latter might come with a video budget that would finance a trip to Australia, a wish shared by Hank. He and Henry had closed the deal on the surf shack, and Henry's boss agreed to let him tend bar a few nights a week at Harry's, just to keep his hand in. Plus, since Jenny and Henry had come to enjoy each other's company, he was smiling often.

Spence was taken with Gus's submersible, and included in his Scripps report a pitch that the Institute invest in its development, and not just because he wanted one. Simon received an enquiry from an entity in the "defense industry" on his possible interest in developing underwater listening devices. He didn't reply, but did Google the home locations of the company's executive board. His new project was above-water electronic ears carried by drones, live streaming of formerly private fireside chats. Tit for tat.

Gloria decided to retire from teaching at the end of the year, and Jack had found a small villa in the mountains near Ojos Negros in Baja, where they would live part time. Simon had commissioned him to build a Velocette Thruxton as a Sunday rider, and Byrnes' Ducati was due for maintenance. Jack felt the comforting Zen of staying off the water for awhile.

Officer Mike, the popular choice for next police chief of Pismo Beach, would come to learn that the singing group of some 400-plus people he had observed through binoculars returned to the pier every year, and stood arm-in-arm in a circle on the beach. Their chant would became a prominent feature of the Clam Festival each fall, with large crowds and network TV coverage. Their message, subliminal in the music, carried to the listeners on hand and those throughout the electronic media. It was a simple missive: Tend to your housekeeping, oppose planetary genocide, you know which way the wind blows. It's a small world after all.

· · ·

Edna hadn't exactly misled the humans on her future plans, but knew that her own methods of interception were learned from the landers, and that they could probably find her with little trouble. Their encryptions would only grow more complex, better to not risk leaving any clues. So she headed for the South China Sea, in the hope that disrupting the latest chest-thumping theatrics of the so-called superpowers could have some effect in modifying their strategies. She would have to make an appearance, since the contenders would simply blame their counterparts for the system malfunctions of the other. She had some work to do on tactics.

She also knew the global war machines would never shut down until their funding was cut off, but held the expectation that regular interruptions of their posturing would at least delay the most deadly incidents. If not by convincing the warriors to take another look at their goals and methods, but giving the citizens the time and information to act on their own behalf. The recent revival among some humans of the odious notion of genetic privilege would require a comprehensive educational campaign, of which she had put Pearl and Jenny in charge. She knew the women would have to lead. As a gender, the males had exhibited little understanding of cause and effect over the years.

Edna was also confident that all the humans with whom she'd connected would make the effort to reform the course of history. She had provided them the information, and the cues on how to use it. They could only grow more aware of how frightening the expanding mutilation of their habitat could become, and the crucial nature of their opposition to it.

She had come to take some pride in her work as an empath, and an enabler, but knew she was hardly a prophet. The humans had obviously made some wonderful achievements for their species over the years, but given their reckless work of the last century, there would be no divining the prospects for this one. Edna held the good thought that they could get it sorted out in time, with or without her help. If not their prospects would be breathtaking. Literally. Choose the reality, she had urged one and all, not the show. Tend the garden you've been given, look after your neighbors.

And thus she set sail, so to speak, for China and new adventures, challenges, languages and friends. The waters of Avila and Pismo would always be home, but she felt their care was now in good hands, and that their degradation might possibly be reversed. She was pleased to hear that the Diablo nuclear plant would soon close. Edna could hear in the distance the songs of gray whales headed south, and chose one of Dugan's favorites to sing her own harmony as she turned west into deep water:

The bottles stand as empty, as they were filled before.
Time there was and plenty, but from that cup no more.
Though I could not caution all, I still might warn a few:
Don't lend your hand to raise no flag atop no ship of fools.
Ship of fools on a cruel sea, ship of fools sail away from me.
It was later than I thought, when I first believed you,
Now I cannot share your laughter, ship of fools.

Postscript

"For the first time in American history, men in authority are talking about an 'emergency' without foreseeable end. Such men as these are crackpot realists: in the name of realism they have created a paranoid reality all their own."

– C. Wright Mills
The Power Elite
1956

Acknowledgments

Thanks to Mike McCarthy, Central Coast History Foundation, Ashala and Brian Lawler, Debra and Toby McKain, Nancy and David Schoonmaker, Ellen and Lance Anderson, Sandy and Chris Sidah, Kathleen Brintnall, John Huetter, Carolyn Knox, Jimmie Ditzel, Tom Robbins, E. L. Doctorow, Rachel Carson, Sue and Clement Salvadori, NPR/KCBX-FM, Sam Sippi, Mitzi Engel, Uncle Adolph, Dennis Pegelow, Virgil Rakestraw, Brian Bennett, Mickey Spillane, Jean Ellison, Bill Schiltz, Jack Baugh, Ron Maruna, Terry Rose, Tom Simmons, Danny Whitten, Lowell George, Lew White and all the twilight ramblers on the road and trail.

The Music

"The High Cost of Living," Jamey Johnson, "That Lonesome Song" album
(Jamey Johnson/James Slater)

"Feelin' Good," Ry Cooder, "Paradise and Lunch" album
(J.B. Lenoir/Jim Dickinson)

"Gone Away," Steve Ripley, "Ripley Ripley" album
(Tim DuBois/Steve Ripley/John Wooley)

"How Can I Live Without You?" Cracker, "The Golden Age" album
(David Charles Lowery/John Hickman)

"Young and Wired," John "Juke" Logan, "The Chill" album
(John Logan)

"Hello in There," John Prine, "John Prine" album
(John Prine)

"Sailin' Shoes," Little Feat, "Sailin' Shoes" album
(Lowell George)

"Southern Cross," Crosby Stills & Nash, "Daylight Again" album
(Michael Curtis/Richard Curtis/Stephen Stills)

"That's It for the Other One," Grateful Dead, "Anthem of the Sun" album
(Jerry Garcia/Bob Weir/Bill Kreutzmann)

"Beyond The Sea," "Sing and Swing with Bobby Darin" album
(Albert Lasry/Charles Trenet/Jack Lawrence)

"Into the Mystic," Van Morrison, "Moondance" album
(Van Morrison)

"Unknown Legend," Neil Young, "Unplugged (Live)" album
(Neil Young)

"The World is What You Make It," Paul Brady, "Miscellaneous" album
(Paul Brady)

"Letting the Days Go By," Talking Heads, "Remain in Light" album
(Brian Eno/Christopher Frantz/David Byrne/Jerry Harrison/
Tina Weymouth)

"Yellow Submarine," The Beatles, "Revolver" album
(John Lennon/Paul McCartney)

"Here Comes the Sun," The Beatles, "Abbey Road" album
(George Harrison/John Lennon/Paul McCartney)

"Let it Be," The Beatles, "Let it Be" album
(John Lennon/Paul McCartney)

"Fields of Gold," Eva Cassidy, "Songbird" album
(Gordon Sumner/Raghupathy Dixit)

"Ship of Fools," Grateful Dead, "30 Trips Around the Sun" album
(Jerry Garcia/Robert Hunter)

About the author

T. J. (Tod Joseph) Rafferty was born in Salem, Ohio, and raised up in Georgia, Florida and northeastern Ohio. A graduate of Kent State University, he has worked in radio, television, advertising, journalism and golf course maintenance. His work has appeared in *Stars and Stripes, Cycle News, Big Bike, Cycle Guide, Motorcyclist, American Roadracing, Robb Report, Cycle World, Moto Euro, New Times, Motorcycle.com* and *RideApart.com*.

His previous books covered the histories of Ducati, Harley-Davidson and Indian motorcycles. This is his first novel. Rafferty and his wife live in a remodeled cave in the La Sal Mountains of southeastern Utah.

A note on the type and printing

The type in this book is *Arno*, an OpenType design by Robert Slimbach of Adobe Systems Incorporated. The chapter titles are set in *Brioso*, another of Slimbach's designs. More calligraphic in nature, the Brioso type is designed to work in concert with Arno.

Mr. Slimbach is the designer of many of the most popular typefaces in modern usage. He has designed, or co-designed at least 19 families of type for Adobe and other foundries.

This book was produced using Adobe *InDesign* and Adobe *Illustrator* on a Macintosh computer. It was printed by BR Printers in San Jose, California.

Copies of this book are available from
Chowderhead Press
San Luis Obispo, California
chowderpress.com

www.ingramcontent.com/pod-product-compliance
Lightning Source LLC
Chambersburg PA
CBHW072117020426
42334CB00018B/1630